CAN'T NOTHING BRING ME DOWN

CAN'T NOTHING BRING ME DOWN

[CHASING MYSELF IN THE
RACE AGAINST TIME]

IDA KEELING

WITH ANITA DIGGS

ZONDERVAN®

ZONDERVAN

Can't Nothing Bring Me Down
Copyright © 2018 by Ida Keeling

Requests for information should be addressed to:
Zondervan, *3900 Sparks Dr. SE, Grand Rapids, Michigan 49546*

ISBN 978-0-310-35143-6 (audio)

ISBN 978-0-310-35064-4 (ebook)

Library of Congress Cataloging-in-Publication Data

Names: Keeling, Ida, 1915- author. | Diggs, Anita Doreen, author.
Title: Can't nothing bring me down : chasing myself in the race against time
/ Ida Keeling with Anita Diggs.
Description: Grand Rapids, Michigan : Zondervan, [2018]
Identifiers: LCCN 2017041065 | ISBN 9780310349891 (hardcover)
Subjects: LCSH: Keeling, Ida, 1915- | Runners (Sports)--United
States--Biography. | Women runners--United States--Biography.
Classification: LCC GV1061.15.K395 A3 2018 | DDC 796.42092 [B] --dc23 LC record
available at https://lccn.loc.gov/2017041065

Cover design: Curt Diepenhorst
Cover photo: Elias Williams
Interior design: Kait Lamphere
Interior background image: © RoyStudio.eu/Shutterstock

First printing December 2017 / Printed in the United States of America

CONTENTS

ACKNOWLEDGMENTS

I'd like to thank my literary agent, Dan Strone;
my collaborator, Anita Diggs; my editor John Sloan;
and my two wonderful daughters, Laura and Cheryl.
But most of all, I owe my greatest thanks to God.

[CHAPTER 1]

SEPTEMBER 1982

When the solution is simple, God is answering. I believe it was a smart man named Albert Einstein who said that. For me, it was my daughter Cheryl who came up with a solution to my problem. If she had not, I would probably be dead today or have a quality of life so low it wouldn't matter if I was alive.

Cheryl dropped by my place one day while I was trying to watch a soap opera. It was hard for me to concentrate because I was feeling so blue. I'm not even sure what soap opera was playing on the screen. Sometimes it seemed like the characters were moving in slow motion and nothing that came out of their mouths made any kind of sense. I guess that's because my psyche had slowed down and it felt like I was moving around in a bowl of thick oatmeal. Not a pleasant feeling, but me and the icky sensation were becoming well acquainted. Too well.

"Mommy, I need a favor," Cheryl said.

"What kinda favor?"

"I want you to go somewhere with me."

Oh no! I didn't feel like getting dressed and going nowhere. It was all I could do to reach out and change the channel on my TV set.

"Cheryl, I'm not up to it."

"Please, Mommy. I really need you to do this."

There was desperation in that please. I turned around to look at her, and my motherly instinct rose up. My baby girl needed my help.

"Okay. I gotta get dressed."

"Oh, we're not going right now. I'll let you know the date."

"Date for what?"

"I need you to go to a cross-country race with me."

I knew all about racing, even though I had never even considered being in a race. Cheryl was a runner and a competitive racer who always told me about her adventures. I enjoyed hearing them but wondered where she got the energy. She had just finished a clerkship for State Supreme Court (Manhattan County) Judge Thomas Dickens and started a fitness business which offered fitness training in the workplace. She also held down a part-time job in real estate and was raising her son, all while running for miles at a time.

But the big question now was why, all of a sudden, Cheryl *needed* me to go to a race with her. What was going on? Was she sick and needed me to be there in case she fainted or something? Was someone stalking her? Lord, have mercy! Was one more of my children at risk?

"Cheryl, what's going on?" I knew my voice sounded shaky as I asked the question, but I just couldn't help it. I had only two children left, and if I lost one or both of my girls, it would be more than my body, mind, and soul could bear. I would just die.

"Mommy, you look like you're about to cry. What's wrong?"

"Something is going on and you're not telling me. Why do you suddenly need me to come see you run?"

She shifted from foot to foot as she figured out how to tell me what she needed to tell me. I never took my eyes off her face.

"No, Mommy. I want *you* to run."

And then I laughed.

"Please, Mommy. Something has to be done about you."

Fall is cross-country running season. That doesn't mean that you run across America. Cross-country just means running outdoors, usually 3.1 miles. It is very different from running indoors. When doing cross-country, you can find yourself running through grass, over a log, and in the rain, with your shoes squishing through mud.

I didn't know any of this when I ran my first race. It was September 1982, and I was sixty-seven years old. I didn't care whether I won the race or not. I didn't care whether I survived it or not. The only reason I was in it was to satisfy my youngest daughter, Cheryl. She was worrying herself to death about me. She now tells people, "The smiles had gone off her face. A light had gone off inside of her. I watched this for eight months after Charles's death. Her appetite wasn't the same. She was lost inside herself. And it just bothered me. Mommy was always on my mind."

Cheryl is right. I was lost. Somebody had tied my eldest son's hands behind his back and then hung him. Nobody had been arrested for the murder. Somebody had beat my other son to death with a baseball bat in broad daylight and no one would step forward to let the police know who did it. The witnesses were too afraid. Telling would mean testifying. Testifying would mean danger to the witnesses' families. There is a saying now in poor communities that "snitches get stitches." My boys were dead, and no one was going to answer for it. The pain was just too much to bear.

It never occurred to me that I would bury even one of my children. It goes against the natural order of things. My children were supposed to stand in a cemetery and watch sadly as my body was lowered into the ground. Not the other way around! It was crazy. Sometimes, even after the funerals and burials, it seemed like none of it could really be true. Both of them had been in the service. War might have broken out and they could have been mortally wounded. That didn't happen. They had survived. Growing up as black, male teenagers in a big-city housing project meant that they had both been at risk every time they walked out of the apartment. They had survived that. They had both lived to marry, father children, and see middle age. I wasn't supposed to be worried about them anymore.

I remember Charles as a baby in my arms, wrapped up in a blue blanket and staring at me. I imagined he was wondering what my next move was gonna be. I thought to myself, *Don't worry, baby boy, Mama is gonna find a permanent home for you.* I knew that would prove to be easier said than done. The real deal is that landlords don't want to hear about cute, chubby babies in warm flannel blankets. They only understand two words: *rent money.* If you don't have it, you have to leave. But I didn't voice my thoughts aloud to my baby even though I knew he couldn't understand a word I was saying. I didn't say it because it's such a hopeless thing to put into a small child's head.

Both my boys clung to me when they were tiny infants. I wish that I would have had more time with them when they were that age, but money was always the most important thing because we had little to none of it. So work came first. Hugs, cuddling, and kisses were in second place, I guess.

Mothers didn't explain what they were doing when my boys were small. Perhaps today a mother might sit her toddler on a chair and say something like, "Now, Timmy. Mommy loves you, but she must go to work to buy you crayons," or something like that. But I come from the "children should just do as they're told" era. I'm not sure one is right over the other, but like anything else, it probably varies from place to place. By place, I mean a house with wealthy parents in it or a house with poor parents in it. Poor parents simply don't have the energy to go into lengthy explanations most of the time. Getting money to eat and pay rent is paramount.

I was a few short years away from my seventieth birthday, and I didn't feel like I needed to be on guard anymore, like I had to try to protect my sons from the evils of the street. I was supposed to be living a life of ease during my retirement. I was supposed to be secure in the fact that my children were going to be just fine. I had watched over them when they needed me to be there, and now they would take care of themselves, right?

Wrong. Two of them were brutally murdered, leaving me to wonder what I could have done differently so that they would have made better choices.

As I grappled with the loss, it occurred to me that no parent is ever really safe. We can never really relax and let our guard down, can we?

I was retired and no longer an employee of any company, so there was no way for me to lose myself in my work after the tragedies by doing every minute of overtime that I could get my hands on.

I tried to remember the agony of losing my mother many years ago and how I got through that. If I could remember the way I got through that pain, would it save me now? There were no answers, and my thoughts just went round and round. I had known a lot of people who had passed on, but thinking about how I managed to move on after those losses did not help me at all. As much as I loved all of those people, I did not give birth to them. This was different. This was some type of hell that I couldn't come to grips with.

It seemed like every time I closed my eyes, I saw one or both of my boys. They were babies in their carriages, which I pushed through the streets of Harlem. Then they were toddlers, the three of us in a homeless shelter until I could find us a home. Then they were running for exercise at the armory, competing with each other and laughing real loud and free. They were sitting in church with me as I warned them not to squirm.

Grown-up Donald drawing remarkably good portraits of people, places, and moods.

Grown-up Charles at the stove, stirring pots while the aroma of the food he was cooking wafted around the room.

Both of them dancing in the living room while their sisters looked on, happy that their older brothers were having a good time.

When Cheryl showed up at my door on the day of the race, I told her to forget the plan because I didn't have any sneakers. She pulled a pair out of her bag.

I squeezed one foot inside. "It feels too snug."

Cheryl's lips tightened and she reached back into her bag. "Try these."

She had come with two pairs of sneakers!

The look on her face told me that she had come prepared for every objection that I might make. It never dawned on her that I might not be able to run 3.1 miles (about sixty-two city blocks) and finish the race. Cheryl probably couldn't afford to let herself think like that because she was determined to save my life.

The race was called the Big Red 5K Mini Run, and it was being held in Brooklyn, New York. *Big Red* was a black newspaper, and they had managed to get more than two hundred people to run. There were many people aged from fifteen to sixty. I was the oldest and probably most reluctant participant. But I ran that first race for my daughter. Just so she would stop looking so worried and scared.

I ran, not knowing what was waiting for me at the end of the road, just as my parents, Osborne and Mary Potter, had done when they left the island of Anegada for America, way back when.

DAY BY DAY

I sit while my mind wonders
about things that used to be
or others that might have been.
So much has passed me by.
All I do is sit and sigh.

CHAPTER 2

WAY BACK WHEN

It has been said that "God will not permit any troubles to come upon us, unless he has a specific plan by which great blessing can come out of the difficulty." My father, Osborne Potter, clearly believed this because he faced one setback after another without losing his stride or even slowing down. An asthmatic since the age of seven, my father was always working. He worked doing physical labor when he first came to America. He worked through the death of my mother, the eviction of our family, and the loss of our grocery store. He was able to keep going because of his firm belief that God knew what was best for him and the rest of us.

My parents were both born and raised on the island of Anegada, a fifteen-square-mile island in the Caribbean. The first people there were called the Arawak and they lived there for hundreds of years in peace until Christopher Columbus saw the island in 1493. You can kinda figure out what happened next, right? Mr. Columbus reported the find back to his bosses in Spain and they claimed the island. Then in 1625, the British took it.

Some years after that, enslaved Africans were forced to come to lots of the Caribbean islands to work on sugar plantations. Many of them were worked to death. That was no problem for their masters. The plantation owners just purchased some more African people to take their places. This went on until 1833 when the British people freed all the slaves in their empire, twenty-nine years before Abraham Lincoln freed the enslaved black Americans.

But Anegada's hard times were not over. In 1853, cholera struck the island and killed almost 15 percent of the citizens. Luckily, my mama and daddy's people survived all of that or I wouldn't be here to tell the tale.

Where my parents came from, food came off the trees and out of the ocean. They had to fish or pick whatever they ate. There were no grocery stores.

Daddy was about five-nine and slim, with a smooth brown complexion, and looked like a Native American. Mama was five feet tall and stout, with light skin and jet-black wavy hair. She was pale because her father was white, a British man named Peter George who settled in Anegada and married a black woman named Zora. They had Mama and three other daughters. Peter George built the Anegada Reef Hotel before the black folk told him to "take his machines and go home." There must be a big story behind that expulsion, but I don't know the details. Zora was left to finish raising her four girls but had plenty of community support. I also don't know why Zora didn't take Mama and her other daughters and go to England with him.

After Mama and Daddy married in 1912, Daddy came to America to work in the navy yard and raise money for her journey. She joined him in late 1913.

Daddy arrived in the United States to find a dangerous kind of racism that he had never known about before. Lynching had become an American epidemic. In many places, lynchings were major public events. People would hear about a lynching coming up and pack food and drink to attend like they were going to a concert or something. In a lot of cases, local law enforcement either turned a blind eye to what was going on or participated in the event. No amount of pleas for mercy, cries of agony, or appeals to God and humanity could stop an excited and eager lynch mob.

Anyway, Mama and Daddy stayed with friends until they found a place to put down roots and raise a family.

Daddy could not grasp the concept of rent. It both fascinated and repelled him. There was no such thing as paying rent on the island of Anegada. Who would pay money each month to own nothing? Of all the American customs he encountered, this one baffled him to the end of his days. Early on, he decided that he would stop paying this thing that Americans called rent as quickly as possible. It would be smarter to become a landlord and collect this rent from anyone foolish enough to participate in such a system.

He and Mama found a place in a New York neighborhood that had originally been called Five Points before the name was changed to Hell's Kitchen.

From early in its history in the mid-1700s, when Hell's Kitchen was known as Five Points, the area already possessed a notorious reputation. Filled with rampant violence, sexual larceny, and crushing poverty, the terrible despair of Five Points' inhabitants was compounded by its having been a dumping ground for the biologic waste of tanneries and slaughterhouses. As new industries arose in the early nineteenth century, new pollutants were added to the toxic mixture. By the Civil War, Five Points stood out as a prime example of the unrelenting obstacles daily confronting its destitute human beings who struggled to eke out meager livings in their cramped, disease-ridden spaces.

Such was the cruel nature of life and the people living in Five Points that, after an 1835 visit, the famous Davy Crockett said that, "In my part of the country, when you meet an Irishman, you find a first-rate gentleman; but these are worse than savages; they are too mean to swab hell's kitchen." The name "Hell's Kitchen" stuck to describe the vice, random violence, large number of murders, and sexual excess of the neighborhood.

However, most of the people who lived in Hell's Kitchen were not criminals; like Mama and Daddy, they were simply poor people who had found a place to settle down and start having babies.

My sister, Omena, came first. She was born in 1914.

I was next, Ida Olive Potter, born in 1915 at home at 239 West 62nd Street. The year I was born was the same year that Southern blacks started migrating to Northern cities in huge numbers. New York City, and especially Harlem, witnessed big changes because of this migration. The people who were coming North certainly had nothing to lose, because the Jim Crow laws where they lived caused them to live in constant stress and fear for their lives. They literally faced spiritual, psychological, emotional, and physical threat every single day. I don't know how all of them didn't just simply go mad. Even though there was plenty of racism and violence against blacks in New York City, it was still less than what they were used to so they came in droves. They soon found out (if they didn't already know) that far from being havens of racial paradise, Northern cities possessed their own tortured history of racial tension and oppression. What happened when they arrived was that some white citizens created a variety of schemes to ensure that blacks did not have access to housing, education, or employment. Real estate compacts, zoning restrictions, and general refusal to rent or sell to blacks reinvigorated the old stresses that had historically characterized the struggles of black folks to survive.

Life in the South had long before become unbearable. Lynching and constant harassment and intimidation, compounded by the lack of education and any foreseeable economic opportunities, made the decision an easy one for millions of blacks. They left the racial hellhole of the South and traveled north to Chicago, Detroit, Cleveland, Indianapolis, and New York. During the year I was born, thousands of black former southerners showed up in Harlem.

Life for blacks in America's Northern cities changed, in some cases for the better. For the most part, though, African Americans were the recipients of Northern versions of Southern hatred. Efforts to move into areas of cities where jobs were plentiful, access to recreational outlets easy, and good housing affordable, were thwarted through elaborate schemes of zoning, renting, and neighborhood compacts that guaranteed blacks would not be able to obtain decent housing.

After me came Oswald, Nollas, Oscar, Daisy, Mary, and Quentin (a girl whom we always called Tina).

From what I understand, we had four rooms: two bedrooms, a living room, and the kitchen. The toilet was in the main hall.

In those days, most babies were born in the house. Doctors came from the nearest hospital and delivered the babies. Birth certificates were sent to the Bureau of Records, then you received your birth certificate through the mail. Roosevelt Hospital was in our neighborhood and close by. There were so many kids coming so fast in our family that when I was only two years old, Daddy moved us to larger apartment on either 63rd or 64th Street. The year was 1917.

Given the back-breaking oppression that black folk were going through, my parents must have been very confused when America and its black citizens went overseas to war with Germany in 1917 to make the world "safe for democracy." Violence because of skin color was a possibility for black folks every single day right there in New York City and the rest of the United States. My parents must have wondered, why go overseas and tell other folk what to do when your own kitchen ain't clean?

One day when I was around three years old, I heard music, loud noise, and laughter coming from outside. I asked my mother, "Mama, what's all that noise?" She said it was Armistice Day. I didn't know anything about Armistice Day or nothing else. So I said, "Armistice Day?" and I walked away. But the music and all got louder. People were out on their fire escapes looking out into the street at the parade. I questioned her further and she said that it meant the soldiers were coming home from the war. I still did not know what she meant but I didn't ask any more questions.

Another memory I have from my early years is an old rocking chair that me and my older sister Omena used to have. My younger brother, Oswald, was in the chair and he was too young to walk so we got on either side of the rocking chair and rocked him. The potato man was downstairs with his horse and wagon singing, "Hobee, boobee, potatoes." So we started singing with the potato man while rocking Oswald back and forth. He loved it.

The kitchen stove operated by a meter above. You put a quarter in and the gas started and the stove worked for one hour. The raw food had to be prepared very carefully in advance because that meter would still be ticking if you had to stop cooking to fix something. In other words, you would be paying even though nothing was cooking. Mama also cut the raw food into very small pieces because it would cook quicker and save some meter time and money for another dish. If the meter cut off while the food was still cooking, you had to have another quarter to feed the meter and finish preparing the meal. No one we knew had quarters to spare. So you had to plan carefully. I remember that meter very well because I would get frightened sometimes when Mama was climbing up on the stool to put in the quarter. It seemed like there were an awful lot of stairs on that stool and I was afraid she was going to fall.

The kitchen also held a big bathtub used for bathing or laundering.

Daddy worked in the navy yard and every payday he would treat us to ice cream cones or pretty socks. When my father used to come home on payday, we didn't know about no payday. We had no idea what a paycheck was or how a person got one. All we knew was that sometimes it was ice cream day. We stayed out on the fire escape gazing up and down the street for signs of Daddy. Looking, looking, looking. Then my sister would holler, "Oh, there's Daddy and he's got the ice cream!" It was so exciting.

Life was different way back when. It moved a lot slower so that a person had time to be in the moment. There wasn't all the rushing around that we have today. Right now, we barely have time to feel or think about one thing before a dozen other things pop up to grab our attention.

Some Sundays Daddy would take us walking to Central Park. We could have taken the bus, but that would have cost fifteen cents apiece, and besides, we needed the exercise. There were no swings or eateries in the park then. Central Park was not built up the way it is now. There was a little pond and some ducks in the water.

When I look back on those walks now, I wish Mama had come along. It seemed to me that she was always washing, cooking, or nursing a baby. It would have been good for her to stroll in the park and stand still for a moment to look at the ducks.

It was during this time that Daddy got pretty excited and talked about buying a building in Harlem. There were a lot of buildings there which had been vacant for a long time. He said that the landlords had built too many houses for sale and there were not enough people living there who wanted to buy property and move into them. So the prices were going down and all he needed were some partners who shared his vision of owning an apartment building.

Mama looked pleased, so Omena and I felt good too.

Mama taught all five of us girls how to sew and I thank God that she did. If I had not learned to sew, I don't know what would have become of me or how I would have supported myself and my children with any kind of dignity.

Daddy gave us our lessons about money. We didn't have a bank so we used Carnation milk cans. After we finished the milk, we used the can opener and opened the can all the way up. Then we washed it out good and that was our bank. When we were small, my father said if you make fifteen cents a week, save a nickel. When we got older, his instructions about how to handle money became more detailed, though the bottom line never really changed. To have money, you had to work very hard doing as many jobs as you could find and then save every cent you could hold on to after the bills were paid.

We never had a birthday party or a Christmas tree or toys. We made our own playthings. For a doll, I took a clothespin, wrapped cloth around it, put it in a baby shoe box, attached a long string to the box, and pulled it up and down the street. We also made beanbags using old socks. The boys all made wagons with wooden boxes, a rope, and wheels, or a scooter on two pieces of wood. The wheels probably came from an old baby carriage or old skates.

One Christmas, Miss Bessie, owner of the restaurant next door, gave me a doll. I felt like I was in heaven because I'd always wanted a doll but there was just no money for such frivolities. The doll was so pretty. Her little pale face had freckles on the cheeks. Her eyes were dark brown and her lashes actually felt like real hair. She had a pink bow at the bottom of each braid. I needed to come up with a name. As I pondered what that name should be, Oswald asked if he could hold her. I generously placed my precious doll in his arms. I had owned her for only about one hour. Oswald was holding it, looking at it, and dropped it. Since these were days before plastic, she broke into many pieces. My body went cold. I couldn't move. For a while it was like I was in mourning. Well, that was my first and last doll.

There was no radio or television. We made our own entertainment and really enjoyed each other's company. With all those kids in a small apartment, there was always something going on . . . singing, teasing, laughing, or watching Oscar clown around.

Mama was very health conscious, although she didn't eat well herself. Mama was not particular about pork or ground beef. She couldn't wash ground beef and had had a bad experience with pork. She made health tonics for us using orange juice, eggs, and milk beaten together. We also had Maltine and cod liver oil every morning. We never had soda, only juice, and not many sweets.

Sometimes Daddy was in a domestic mood. At those times, he would always make the best fricassee chicken and dumplings and a nut cake. Those were fun evenings. After dinner, he would play with us, swing us around, and the rest of the family clapped happily.

Since I was his second-born child, Daddy called me Deuce. One time, Mama was gone overnight. The next morning, I asked Daddy where she was.

"In the hospital, Deuce," was his reply.

I considered this for a moment. "When is she coming back?"

"Next week."

So I ran to the window and stayed there, looking up and down the street.

Finally, he said, "Deuce, what you looking for?

"I'm looking for next week, Daddy."

He laughed long and hard.

Since all of my brothers and sisters were born at home, Mama couldn't have been having a baby. I never learned what the mysterious illness was that kept her away for that whole week.

Soon it was time for me to start school. As a small child, I had been told that the white man on the cross was God and that God loved all people and that people went to church to thank God for his love and protection.

I started school in 1921 and the teacher was white. Her name was Miss Tilson and I felt good that she was white like God.

I had no knowledge of reading or writing. At home, we had no children's books, crayons, pencils, or paper of any kind except the *Daily Sun*, so reading and writing were new things for me. I had a hard time with both so the teacher asked one of the children to place a hand over mine in order to guide me through those strange symbols. As long as the child's hand was over mine, I did just fine. The second day, I had to do it alone and I found making twos and threes very difficult. Miss Tilson slammed my elbow on the desk so hard that I saw stars. A pain went through my body that hurt so bad, I have never been able to put it into words.

That evening, with tears in my eyes, I told Mama. She couldn't go to the school because she had too many babies. She didn't feel well as she was tired, pregnant, and had to prepare lots of things for the next day. Daddy was still working at the navy yard. I felt I had nowhere to turn. I didn't have anyone to come to school to complain. I had always sucked my finger whenever I was nervous. After one week in school, my finger became my constant companion.

Back when I started school, hitting children, or corporal punishment as they called it, was not illegal. In fact, parents believed that since teachers were adults, children had to learn how to get along with them and not the other way around. Teachers were adults, and adults could hit. Add to that, the fact that most poor and uneducated parents were in awe of the teacher simply because she had been to college, and you had a situation where the child had no voice or recourse when a teacher lost control. Some of the reluctance of parents to come to school might have also had a religious base. Proverbs 23:13–14 does say, "Do not withhold discipline from a child; punish him with the rod and save his soul from death" (NIV 1984).

It took a lot for a teacher to get fired for physically attacking a child, and most of the time, unless the teacher's actions could have resulted in almost certain death, school administrators simply did not care. But I did not understand any of this at the time.

Thereafter, I spent a lot of my time trying not to say or do anything that would make Miss Tilson hurt my arm anymore. That time would have been better spent actually learning something. In any case, she did not attack me again. Even if she had, I would not have said anything to Mama or Daddy. What would have been the point? If Mama didn't come and give the teacher a stern warning the first time, I had no reason to believe that she or Daddy would do anything about Miss Tilson hitting me in the future. By the time my own kids came along, teachers who ruled by hitting were frowned upon. Miss Tilson also abused other children. Some parents did come in and some did not. She was fired after choking a Spanish boy. His mother came to school the next day and there were red hairpins everywhere because the child's mother had snatched them right out of the teacher's hair.

Mama and Daddy were always busy. He was usually at the navy yard. She was doing household chores with a bunch of kids around her ankles. It would have been hard for her to get away to pick me up from school. So my parents asked for help. Because of this, I got lost one day. This girl who lived in my building was supposed to pick me up on her way home from school and take me with her. What happened was when I got downstairs, she was with her friends. I was a slow walker. She said, "Come on." I couldn't keep up and she said, "I'm not waiting for you." I tried to watch to see which way she was going, and all of a sudden, she disappeared. I just kept walking and a policeman stopped me and said, "Little girl, where are you going? Where do you live?" My answer was, "With Mama and Daddy." He continued, "What is your address?" I didn't know my address because the little girl was going to do the picking up, the taking home. She had been nice when her parents were around. After that she turned into Miss Nasty because her friends were watching.

The policeman walked me back to the school and my parents were summoned to come get me.

I had never been so glad to see them.

Meanwhile, Daddy had been busy trying to become a land-lord instead of a renter. In 1921, he went into a partnership with two Italian guys. The three of them bought an apartment build-ing at 2473 Seventh Avenue in Harlem. One day a big truck came and took everything out of our apartment. Daddy put us in a cab to the new neighborhood. There were tree-lined streets, pretty buildings with curtains on the glass doors, and shiny mailboxes and doorknobs. There were upholstery awnings at the windows to keep the sun out. We moved into a spacious six-room apart-ment and stayed there for three years before a falling-out between the partners forced us to move. You see, the partners' families did not live in the building, yet Daddy had a free apartment. They felt he was getting more out of the building than they were and decided to buy him out. We had to find a new place to live.

Mama told him, "Bunn, don't get no more partnerships," but he did not listen.

So, when I was nine years old, Daddy decided to buy another house. He found another partnership with two other guys. Mama was not pleased with the idea and told him so, but he continued on with his plans. Daddy was the undisputed head of our household and women didn't have much of a voice in a family's financial affairs back in those days. Mama had to go along with whatever he decided to do even if she could see disaster looming ahead. It had to be very frustrating for her and I'm glad that things have changed for women.

The three men found a house and bought 287 West 142nd Street, another Harlem building, and we moved into an apart-ment there. It was a cold-water flat with no steam heat. Daddy talked about converting the building to heat and hot water. Mama said, "Osborne, don't do that." Even though it was uncomfortable, Mama told him not to make a change until he could afford to do it on his own. "Leave it a cold-water flat until you are the sole owner," she said.

"You never worked a day in your life, what do you know?" he replied. Again, he did not listen. Daddy told Tantee (that's my aunt on my mother's side) that it would cost five thousand dollars to convert the building to steam heat.

That was a lot of money. Even split three ways between the partners, it meant that Daddy's share would be $1,666. I don't know where he got the cash. Had he saved that much money? Did he borrow it from someone? If so, how did he ever pay it back?

Thinking back from where I am now, he should have listened to Mama. It was the wrong time to purchase a house and then to convert it. Well, I guess he thought he could.

Our apartment was on the main floor. It was nice. Five rooms, a private hall, good closet space, bigger rooms, and Mama could look out windows and see something besides clotheslines and fire escapes. The windows were three sets of bay windows right off the street. Mama made crisscross curtains. The apartment looked good. We were all moving right along.

Mama had no choice but to let Daddy do what he wanted to do even as the conversion went forward. Besides, she had her hands full cleaning and cooking for all of us. We usually had oatmeal and prunes for breakfast. We came home for lunch, which was leftovers from dinner the night before. Our after-school snack was johnnycake, which was whole-wheat flour and water cooked on top of the stove. Dinner was either lamb stew, beef stew, beans and rice, or chili con carne, but on Sunday there was pot roast. We didn't have much chicken. My sister Mary calls Mama "the original health nut." We had lots of fish, fresh fruit, and vegetables. Always more fruit and vegetables than meat or dairy. After all, in Anegada, the fruits and vegetables came from the trees and out of the ground. The fish was caught fresh from the water; there were no snacks, candy, or soda on the island, so my parents did not know any other way to live. These were the habits Mama and Daddy brought with them. I guess that my siblings and I had an Anegadian upbringing on American soil.

One time, money was so tight for a month that food became scarce in our house because there were so many people to feed. A neighbor gave Mama a piece of fresh pork to roast. Mama didn't want it because neither she nor my father believed in eating pork, but she was not about to let her family go hungry. She tried to follow the neighbor's instructions, but I guess she did something wrong because everyone in the house got sick and had to get treated in the emergency room. After that, I never saw pork in our house again, no matter how bad times got.

The three youngest children (Daisy, Mary, and Tina) were all born in the hospital. Daddy went to get Mama from the hospital one day. When they came back, she had a baby named Daisy. The baby was real pretty with a lot of curly hair. I was not accustomed to Mama going away and coming back with a baby because all the rest of us had been born at home, so I was very confused about the whole thing.

While my parents wrestled with our economic problems, my siblings and I dealt with our own concerns. By now, all of us older kids were in school and dealing with the problems that all kids have. How to get good school reports, how to make friends, and things like that. Mama and Daddy were always busy so we pretty much figured out those kinds of things by ourselves.

Later on, I got my first best friend, a Panamanian girl named Estelle. We spent our time jumping double Dutch, skating, racing, and climbing trees. Once, a group of five neighborhood kids chipped in and hired a bike for a quarter. We took turns riding it all day. It was so much fun.

At one point, my siblings and I all had our own friends. This led to squabbles about who didn't like who until Daddy got tired of hearing it and said, "Whether you like their friends or not, that's their friends. I don't want to hear no argument."

With so many kids in the house, there were always two having a disagreement about something. Mama would let the two parties vent for a little while before she stepped in and made a decision about who was right and who was wrong. Her decision was final and we learned very quickly to let the issue slide once she had spoken. If Daddy heard anything else, he would come stomping out of their room and yell, "Listen to your mama. I don't want to come out here anymore."

Tina was born when I was ten and she was like a doll for me to play with; I made sure that Tina was never wet or hungry. Since there was such a huge age difference between us, we didn't really become friends until adulthood. But before that, she was my baby. I made her first dresses and fussed over her like she was my own child. She was fun, unlike Mary who was a sickly child.

Mary had sprue which is a chronic digestive disorder. It seemed like whatever Mama gave her to eat came right back up or made her stomach cramp. She lost weight at the drop of a hat and was extremely skinny because there was so little food that she could eat and hold onto. She was also a nervous wreck. A sudden loud noise would upset her. A prolonged argument would upset her. You certainly couldn't tease her or get into any kind of argument with her. I felt sorry for Mary. Her life seemed exhausting. For some reason, sprue usually affects people of Caribbean descent. Later on, Mary was sent to Catholic school because public school was too rough for her constitution.

A year after buying the second Harlem building, Daddy got further into debt when he bought a grocery store at 2187 Seventh Avenue between 129th and 130th Street. So now he was a landlord and a business owner. He was one hardworking man.

My brother Oswald and I worked in the store. Everything came in a croker sack, like the grits and the sugar and the rice. A croker sack looks like a burlap bag, but it's coarser and stronger. There was a scale to weigh one pound, three pounds, and five pounds because that's what people would ask for. People mostly bought three pounds of everything. We also had milk. The milk came in two big chrome galvanized containers. There was the pint and the quart. Everybody bought their milk pail and it cost two dollars a quart. The bread man came twice a day. Fresh bread came in the morning and sold for eight cents. By noon it wasn't considered fresh bread anymore. The bread man would come back and take it out and give you another tray. He took the old tray to a bakery and they would sell it for a penny a loaf.

Daddy had realized his dreams of home ownership and was extremely proud that he was now a self-employed man, but he had moved a little too fast and was in way over his head. Things started going bad after a while, so he started taking money from the store to keep the apartment building going, but it didn't work.

When this second partnership was dissolved, he couldn't keep up the apartment building payments. As a result, we lost our home. We had to live in the back of the store. There were three big rooms back there. A partition divided the only bedroom so that it made two small bedrooms. There was only one closet. The whole apartment looked like a dormitory housing six children and two adults, with another baby on the way. The apartment was designed to accommodate someone while they worked in the store, not for heavy family living. The only room that did not have a bed in it was the kitchen. Before we left that place for a new apartment, there were two more babies, bringing the grand total to eight children. In just about three years, I had lived in three different places and attended three different schools. I did not understand or care about broken business deals, disgruntled partners, or people whose ambition exceeded their means. I just wanted to stay in one place.

Nevertheless, I loved living in back of the store. We had access to the back yard and used to play a game there with a tire which was tied around a tree. We also had a fire escape to play on.

My new classroom was crowded, just like the house. In those days, there were no laws about how many kids could be stuffed into one classroom. Overcrowding was real, but no one talked about it, and the teachers must have felt overwhelmed at times. Most of the children in my class came from families that did not have any more money than mine had. This was a blessing because I was a sensitive child who would have noticed the difference and felt badly even though I never would have said a word about it.

I started playing hooky, although I didn't know then what it was that was driving me. I only remember feeling squeezed.

It seemed like there wasn't enough space nowhere. At home, we were shoulder to shoulder even at night, because there were too many of us for everyone to have his own bed. During the day, the classroom was often overcrowded and I eventually found myself wishing for a space to just be. I would walk past the school and go down by the East River, sit on my books, and watch the river move ever so calm. Sometimes a log would go by, never no garbage.

We were still living on Seventh Avenue, which was considered the black folks' Broadway. Blacks owned most of the small businesses and a few of the buildings. I remember three little gray shops that were restaurants. Blue/White Diamond Jewelers on 125th Street was also black owned, but the owner had to put white management in to draw the black customers. No one knew that the owner was black until after he died.

It was a vibrant scene. Apex hair dressing/training school was on 135th Street, and above that was the space which Percy Sutton would someday claim for his law office before going on to become one of the most famous and respected men in the history of Harlem.

Most of the black doctors owned their buildings, especially on Strivers Row which was right off Seventh Avenue. Closer to home, there was the famous Lafayette Theater, the chicken & waffle house, and Count Basie and his band also had space nearby.

I remember 1927 when the street lights were put in. The school teachers took the students out and warned them to cross only on the green light, never on the red or anything in between. I also remember when they started building the Independent Subway line back in 1932 and the Eighth Avenue El train being taken down around 1936.

Someone started a wet wash service. They would pick up your clothes and return them a day later in a big canvas bag. That was a big help to Mama who had another baby on the way. Sleeping arrangements were as follows: In one of the bedrooms was Mama, Daisy, and Mary, who was the youngest. In the other small bedroom was Omena, myself, and Oscar. In the living room we had a divan. Daddy and others slept there.

The store continued to do well, but the way things were sold started to change.

Fresh bread and milk were still delivered to the store every day, and the day-old bread and cake were still taken away. But the milk now came in larger metal containers. The small one held about four gallons. The large one held about ten gallons. There was a pint-size dipper in the small one and a quart-size dipper in the large one. People brought in their milk pail every morning. The cheese came wrapped in cheesecloth in a big round container about thirty-eight inches in circumference and six inches tall and then it was cut to order. Rice, sugar, flour, cornmeal, and grits came in fifty-pound burlap bags and had to be weighed in one and two-pound paper bags and stored under the counter, ready for sale as customers came into the store. No more croker sacks.

Daddy was having asthma attacks more frequently. Oswald had to keep the store clean and weigh up the bags of sugar, rice, and flour. I folded them and stored them under the counter. On Saturdays, Oswald and I took grocery orders over the phone and delivered them. We traveled from the store to as far as ten blocks away carrying groceries in corrugated boxes on our shoulders. We held onto the boxes with one hand on our hip, and walked down from 129th Street to 118th Street. Or we went uptown into the 130s. This was continuous for three hours on Saturdays, rain or shine. People gave us two or three-cent tips, but Daddy took our tip money. He'd say, "How much you got?"

"Well, Daddy, I got three cents and Oswald got three cents."

"Yeah," he replied, "put it on the counter."

So we put it on the counter and he took it.

I said, "Daddy, that's our money."

He said, "That's my groceries."

We felt bad about that. Oswald would go next door to the shoemaker and shine shoes for nickels and dimes. I would clean up for one of our favorite customers or mind her little girl, Gloria. This drive to work continued throughout our teens and beyond.

I took my new baby sister, Tina, as my own personal doll. Now there were ten of us in these rooms. The grocery store continued to do well. I think business was booming everywhere. People were always dressed up and looking happy. Things were going good for the Potter clan. Then one day there were a lot of confused looks on people's faces. There was a lot of talk about Wall Street and the stock market. People were jumping out of office windows. The paper boys were yelling, "Extra! Extra! Read all about it!" People stopped in the street to listen because a man was yelling like it was very important that some big stock market had crashed. In the coming days, people jumped off the Empire State Building so often that for a while it was called Suicide Point.

The stock market crash happened on October 29, 1929, which was Mama's forty-first birthday. The Great Depression had begun.

Things started going downhill and bad times lasted for many, many years.

Like the rest of the United States, the 1929 stock market crash jolted Harlem. The economic devastation that swept the nation gripped black folk mightily because we also had racism to deal with. Grown men fought over scraps. Sixty-three percent of the children in Harlem struggled with malnutrition. With the onset of the Great Depression, the desperation of millions compounded blacks' usual difficulties in securing and maintaining employment and providing for their families.

When the Great Depression came, our customers didn't have any more money to buy stuff. People were without their basic needs. Daddy had to pull money from the store to pay for the house at 287 West 142nd Street. Then we moved to a railroad flat that had heat and hot water, and what did Daddy do? He took out the gas stove and put in a coal stove and bought one bag of coal. After the coal was gone, we had to get warm the best way we could. Daddy had no extra money in the store because he had spent it all trying to keep that last apartment building afloat.

Daddy lost the store and our family hit rock bottom. He rented a wooden pushcart and rolled it through the streets, selling fruits and vegetables. We moved again to another cold-water flat, only this time there was no money for coal or wood to keep us warm.

Daddy lost everything but never gave up. He took the push cart and went up to the Bronx wholesale market and filled his cart with onions, potatoes, cabbage, spinach, string beans, and lemons. After he got the pushcart, we ate most of what he couldn't sell, like cabbage and white potatoes, which Mama made with boiled spareribs. He and Oswald pushed up and down streets selling wherever they could. Daddy finally found a spot on Lenox Avenue and 139th Street. By the time Daddy found it, Oswald was no longer with him. They had a disagreement because Oswald rented a cart too and bought supplies from the wholesale market. Daddy was furious and told Oswald, "Whatever money you make on this cart, you give it to me." Oswald said no. He had gotten the cart and supplies with his own money. Daddy said, "There is only one man here and that is me." Oswald still refused to give him the money, so Daddy said Oswald could no longer stay at the house.

Oswald went to Mr. Rose's house. He was the shoemaker and our neighbor when we had the store. He told Mr. Rose what happened. Mr. Rose told Oswald he could stay in his basement. Mr. Rose owned the six-story building on the corner of 129th Street, so that's where Oswald stayed and continued to rent his cart and go the other way. One day, while pushing around, he met Aunt Tantee and explained what happened. She invited him to stay with her. She had three bedrooms and was alone since her daughter had passed away. So Oswald stayed with her until he got called for the merchant marine in July of 1934.

The weather was getting bad, but we could not find any wood to burn in the stove since most of the buildings on the block were using coal. My brother, Oscar, pulled a door off one of the rooms and busted it up for fire. He did this more than once. When he ran out of room doors, he used cabinet doors and drawers. Years later, when we prepared to move yet again, the landlord was furious.

In 1935, we moved to a six-room apartment. Daddy's pushcart was doing pretty good. Daisy and I helped him most weekends and during summer vacations. She would be with Daddy most of the time.

Estelle was still my closest girlfriend. She lived with her father and grandmother who worked all kinds of hours. I'm not sure what had happened to her mother, but her father was overly strict and kind of mean. They lived in the building next to mine. One day, Estelle and I had come home from school. I started into my house, and I saw her start into her place and then stop.

I called out, "What happened?"

She said, "I can't find my key."

I went to her and said, "Don't worry."

She said, "I'm so afraid. I'm going to get a whipping."

Now, Estelle lived on the fourth floor of her building. I had an idea. What if I somehow got onto her fire escape, went into her apartment through the window, and got the keys for her? It seemed like a sound plan to me. So I went up to the fourth floor of my building and asked the woman who lived there if I could go out on her fire escape.

The woman said, "You could get hurt."

I replied, "Just pray for me," and went out her window.

By this time, Estelle was standing in the hallway.

I knew that if I misstepped, I would end up crumpled on the concrete ground between our two buildings, but I had no fear. I just kept my mind on Estelle's need for somebody to help her. I climbed over and onto her fire escape. Those windows were always kept open. I had to take my foot and push up the window. Then I went through feet first and fell onto Estelle's floor.

I quickly made my way through the apartment. I went through a living room and then toward the front of the place.

Right next to the front door there was a table with a lamp on it. Estelle's keys were right there. I grabbed them and went back to the window, onto the fire escape, and into the neighbor woman's house. I didn't go out through the door because I was afraid I'd be seen and my parents would find out. I don't know if the neighbor woman had been praying like I had asked her to or not, but she sure looked relieved to see me.

"You didn't cut yourself and leave any blood over there, did you?"

I gave her a quick smile. "No, there is no blood over there. Here I am, just fine.

Then I ran past her, out her door, down the stairs, and out into the street.

Estelle was standing right there in front of the building. She had her hands up to her face.

I asked, "What is the matter with you?"

She said, "I'm just so afraid."

Weeks later, Estelle's father heard about the whole affair. I had told my friend Dorothy who lived on the main floor of Estelle's building. She told her father who relayed the story to Estelle's father.

He caught up with me one afternoon and told me, "You didn't have to do all of that."

I said, "I didn't want Estelle to get no beating because she forgot her keys."

He said, "She wouldn't have got no beating."

I said, "I couldn't take that chance. She is my best friend."

So he said, "Well, thank you very much. I'm so happy that you made it. Please don't try that again. Next time Estelle forgets her keys, let her stay at your house till I come home."

Luckily for me, nobody ever told my parents.

WINTER BLUES

Looking out of my window in silence
watching the violent wind blowing snow
in all directions.
The freezing rain turns snow into a
mass of ice.
With fears of slipping or falling.
Then it happens.
Heels in the air.
Flat on my back wondering how
I got there.
I was being so careful.
It was also embarrassing.
After taking all the time to
get back on my feet
brush myself off
the first step I took.
Oops!
Down again
No telling when it will end.

CHAPTER 3

FROM SCHOOL TO WORK

Second Timothy 2:6 says, "The hardworking farmer should be the first to receive a share of the crops." I guess something like that was going through my mind when I was confronted with the graduation requirements at school. I suppose I figured that since I had worked so hard at the store, I could get just a tiny crop in order to graduate. Boy, was I wrong.

I was a student at Textile High School in the Chelsea district of Manhattan. According to the Board of Education, the school was established in 1922 to meet the educational needs of the leading industry of the city. Apparently, New York City was the largest distribution and selling point of textiles in the world. Textile High School was the first technical high school devoted to a single industry. There was a textile mill in the basement and the school yearbook was titled *The Loom*. I took regular courses but also did charity work, which consisted of making nurses' uniforms or gym suits for Catholic school students. We also made lots of other garments to prepare for work in the industry.

The teachers gave you a mark which reflected the quality and quantity of your work. I did very well on zippers, collars, and sleeves. My marks were good in terms of sewing. I just didn't care about many other subjects that were part of the curriculum, like science. I wanted to get the basics of sewing down pat so I could get an operating job. Otherwise, school was turning into a drag.

First of all, I was wearing a junior-high school uniform because I didn't have money to buy a new one. It was a blue skirt and white middy blouse. I discarded the black tie but couldn't do anything about the middy blouse which no one else at Textile High School was wearing. My outfit caused me to get teased, ridiculed, and pointed at by giggling girls almost every single day. Fashionably challenged though I was, I was determined to study and become better than those who looked down upon me for what I wore in my impoverished state. Yes, I was hurt, but I still wanted as much abundance for them as I wanted for myself. That is what I felt and believed that God would want me to do.

I didn't have any money to improve my wardrobe or to buy just one meal at school, which I wanted very badly. For lunch every day, I ate a peanut butter sandwich that I brought from home. There was no money to buy a cafeteria lunch because all I had was ten cents for the round-trip carfare. One day, the smell of all that good cafeteria food just consumed me. I couldn't resist. So I spent my five cents for a bowl of mashed potatoes with gravy. Having spent my carfare, I had to walk home from Thirteenth Street and Sixth Avenue to 144th Street, near Bradhurst Avenue. With every step, I regretted my impulsive decision even though the meal had been very tasty. The walk home was 145 blocks and I arrived home three hours later than I normally did. I was cold, hungry again, and tired. The family had already eaten and there was no dinner left for me because no one knew where I was. It seemed to me that it shouldn't have mattered where I was. They knew I was going to come home at some point. They were just greedy and had eaten my share. I wasn't fooled a bit. I curled up on the bed with all my clothes on and went to sleep.

It was almost time to prepare for graduation that was coming up in a few months. We had to make something special. Our choices were to either sew a coat with fur or a tunic with a matching skirt. I decided to create the tunic because it was cheaper to make. I was excited about the project when I approached Daddy.

"Daddy, can I talk to you?"

He looked up from whatever writing he was doing and smiled. "Sure, Deuce. What is it?"

"I need eight dollars for school."

He frowned and shook his head from side to side. "What?"

"I have to sew a garment to graduate and get my high-school diploma."

"Why does this cost so much money?"

"Because I have to buy the material from Canal Street."

"I don't have it," he said flatly.

"Please, Daddy. I really need the money or I can't do the project."

"Did you hear what I just told you?"

Tears of shock and frustration filled my eyes and spilled down my cheeks. I was so shocked because I used to help Daddy with the cart and he would promise to pay me four dollars. Most of the time I didn't get it, but this time I really needed the eight dollars to finish high school.

He turned back to his paperwork and the conversation was over.

How could he leave me hanging like that without even trying to raise the money for me? Wasn't he proud that I even cared about graduating?

Because I couldn't come up with the money to make the tunic, I couldn't march with my class. Instead of getting to graduate and receive a real high-school diploma, they gave me a certificate. I tore it up because I had worked so hard at my studies and didn't get a chance to show what I could do. It seemed so unfair, and I was upset about it for many years.

There were still a few weeks of school left, but instead of going to school the next day, I decided to just go and get a job. It was not like I was going to be allowed to graduate anyway.

It was not unusual for children of the 1930s to leave high school before graduating. Many had to quit school and help work to support their families during the Depression. Others were just anxious to be grown-ups. And many never entered high school in the first place. After all, there were no laws back then that said you had to go to school until you reached a certain age or your parents would get into trouble. Since I didn't know a whole lot of people who had graduated from high school, I didn't really think about the effect not having a high school diploma would have on my life. If I had, maybe I would have just asked Daddy to transfer me to another school—one without a graduation project that he would have to pay for. I didn't know anyone who was my age and even thinking about entering college. Could I have finished high school and worked my way through some little college out of New York by sewing for people? I never even thought of the idea, and

I'm not sure if scholarships or financial aid of any kind was even available at the time.

It is a weird case. I didn't drop out because I was on drugs, alcohol, hated school, or because I was pregnant and being asked to leave. I dropped out because of disappointment. It has occurred to me now that maybe if I had told the school principal why I was leaving, maybe the administration would have taken up a collection to raise the eight dollars for me. Or is that just my imagination? Times were so bad that they probably didn't even notice when one tiny girl just walked away.

One thing is for sure: a high-school diploma wouldn't have done me one bit of good in the factories. It wouldn't have gotten me a job as head of the factory or foreman. That job was almost always held by a man and they certainly weren't going to have no black woman bossing all those people around. I don't think I ever saw a single black woman running anything that she didn't own.

So, I guess it comes down to the question of how my life would have been different if I had finished high school and found a way to go to some Negro college in the South. Would I have met and married some safe boy whose family didn't mind him getting mixed up with a girl of West Indian descent? Maybe I would have become a teacher.

I wish that Textile High School would have had school psychologists to help me cope with the disappointment or, better yet, after-school jobs where I could have earned the eight dollars.

Young people today do not realize that they have resources available to them that we could never have dreamed about. This was long before the civil rights movement, student rights movement, hippie movement, Great Society programs, or any other kind of way for a wrong to be addressed in any kind of real way. Either your parents had the means and the desire to push you ahead or you somehow got out in the world and made your own way the best you could.

When I became a mother, I stressed education above everything else. But when I was growing up, legally obtained money trumped school. My siblings and I were trained to be business (money) minded and independent from an early age. I remember Omena would go to the wholesale place and get men's socks and handkerchiefs and sell them on Saturdays after working in the factory all week. I would relieve her for a few hours each Saturday. All of the sisters sewed their own clothes to save money on store-bought garments. In those days, almost everybody learned to sew because material was cheaper than buying ready-made clothes. We were all petite so we had to alter almost everything. We bought or remodeled every single outfit, and all of us worked in a factory at one time or another. We all tried to have a hidden nest egg, so when I started working, I tried to save a dollar out of every paycheck.

Going to work turned out to be so different from going to school that the year went by faster. I also felt like I got old quicker. After leaving high school because I wasn't properly dressed, I got into the habit of walking a great deal every day to ease my sorrow. One day, I had walked a very long way before I looked up at my surroundings. I felt tired when I realized that I was in a strange neighborhood. I noticed a sign in a candy store window that read "Girl Wanted." I thought, *Oh boy, a job!* So I went inside. There was an old man and a young woman just sitting there.

The old man was fat and had sparse red hair on his big round head. He wore glasses with round frames and peered at me but said nothing. The girl had dark hair and looked Spanish. She could not have been much older than I was.

"May I help you?" she asked.

"I'm here about the job. Your sign says, 'Girl Wanted.'"

"Yes. We need help behind the counter. Get started."

"But I don't know what to do."

"Stay here with Papa. I have to go home, but I'll be back soon. I'll show you the job then."

So she was his daughter. Boy, was I surprised. They didn't look anything alike. She left before I could think of what to say next so I took off my coat and went behind the counter. The daughter had not been gone five minutes when he pointed his finger in my direction.

"Take off your clothes."

"What?"

"I said take off your clothes."

I grabbed my coat and left that candy store so fast I forgot my cap.

When I think about the incident now, it makes me shiver and wonder if the store was just a front. Perhaps they weren't really selling candy at all. Maybe it was an enterprise that lured broke young girls inside and then forced them into prostitution. Not one family member knew where I had gone walking that day. Poor, dumb me could have been snatched or sold off and never seen again. After that, I tried to always let someone know where I was headed.

The next day I went down to the factory district to get whatever work I could.

I didn't have enough speed experience on the sewing machine, because in school speed didn't count. Quality did. I tried many factories that day, even those that did not have a help wanted sign outside. It was the only way to gain experience and pick up factory speed while looking for a better job. But I was turned away because they had no openings.

I finally saw another "Girl Wanted" sign. This was a job which mainly consisted of running errands and paid six dollars a week. I took it to accumulate some money. When I wasn't running errands, I helped make fancy buttonhole looks and then delivered them to Rockaway, Brooklyn, the Bronx, and Manhattan. I had no idea what to expect as a worker in someone else's company. The only real work experience I had was helping out in Daddy's store, which was not the same as punching a time clock or having a set lunch hour.

At home, everyone was delighted that I was going to work. No one noticed or cared about my thwarted high-school graduation. I was going to earn money and bring some of it into the house. That was all that mattered. There was no point in complaining to Mama because, even if she agreed with me, my father's decision was the only one that mattered. There was no point in going back to him, because he hated having to explain himself on a subject more than once. It made him really angry. There was no point in complaining to my older sister, Omena, because at that point in her life (she would later change), money meant a lot more to her than a piece of paper which said that you had read some books.

I brooded about the lost diploma when I had time to myself. Sometimes, I would let my imagination run ahead of me a little bit. I would picture myself coming down the aisle of the auditorium and filing into the reserved student seats with the rest of my class. I would see the beaming faces of my parents and siblings as they sat down and looked eagerly around for me. I would hear my name being called and then watch (in my mind's eye) my legs stroll toward the podium. Then (in slow motion), the principal would hold up my diploma which had a red bow tied around it for all to see before placing it in my eager little hand. The fantasy didn't stop there. I clutched the precious paper and looked from side to side with a big old smile on my face as I went back toward my seat. Before I reached it, Mama and Daddy leaned over and grabbed the hem of my brand new white dress. As they held onto the piece of my garment, I heard them whisper, "We are proud of you, Ida."

When I started that first job, I found it hard to concentrate on the task in front of me because the whole world around me was just so new. There were people who spoke languages that didn't sound familiar to me at all. Plus, in school you could raise your hand and go to the bathroom or get water if you wanted. In the factory, break times were rigid. Unless you were sick, there was no way to do either of those things unless it was break time. In my daddy's store, I could see the sun, the rain, and people walking to and fro, going on about their lives. In the factory, there was no way to know what the weather was like outside. You were in this enclosed space, and most of the time, the windows were way above my head. This was no accident. They didn't want people day dreaming while looking out the window. Factory workers had to concentrate on the piece of fabric in front of them at all times. Just looking up and rubbing your neck was likely to get a questioning stare from the manager. That first day, it didn't take long for my eyes and neck to get tired. But I instinctively knew that reporting my ailments to the manager was not likely to end well for me. So I kept my head down, eyes glued to the garment.

When I was told that I had to go outside to make deliveries, I almost leapt for joy. I didn't mind the traveling, and my day seemed shorter.

WINTER'S DECORATION

The fallen snow upon bare
branches.
Icicles hanging from buildings
below.
Missing are leaves that danced in the
breeze.
While birds happily sang in the
trees.

[CHAPTER 4]

STANDING ON MY OWN TWO FEET

Psalm 147:3 says, "He heals the brokenhearted and binds up their wounds." I was about to get some all-too-direct experience with heartbreak and wound binding.

At nineteen, I worked in a factory and at any other odd jobs that I could find. I didn't go out that much and never on dates. We did things as a group instead of being paired off. It was 1934 and we were still living through the Great Depression. Money was a constant worry. My brothers, sisters, and friends were always trying to work by babysitting, washing windows, or mopping up for somebody. The going wage was only twenty-five cents a day. That is all we got paid.

Once, I was keeping two children, taking them out every day and then bringing them back around dinner time, and I got twenty-five cents each time. Often, their mother didn't have the money after I had worked all day. I kept taking the kids out until she owed me six whole dollars. I said to myself, *This is too much, I'm overdoing it. She is taking advantage of me. She probably thinks that I'm a fool.* Six dollars was a lot of money back then. It was time to have a powwow.

When I approached her, she looked up and gave me the type of benevolent smile that people bestow on toddlers before patting them gently on the head.

"I need the money you owe me. I can't keep minding your babies for nothing."

"Ida, you just have to wait. I can't help you none right now."

"We need to get this fixed today."

"I tell you what, I'll get another girl to keep the kids. How about that?"

"My mother is in the hospital and I would like to go see her. Can't you give me at least *some* of the six dollars?"

"No. I don't have it."

"Okay."

I went home steaming, but it didn't occur to me that she would really hire someone else.

The next day I showed up and she had a new girl already. The new girl was holding the baby who was about two or three years old. I grabbed the baby by her foot and said, "Hi, Joyce, how you doin?" The new girl ran upstairs and told the mother I hit the kid, but I didn't know that at the time. When I saw there was a new girl, I went back home and started thinking about getting another odd job to take the place of the one I had just lost.

I was sitting outside my house and all of a sudden here comes these two white guys. One of them was holding a long piece of paper and the boys on my block stopped playing ball when they saw him. The white guy came over to me and asked, "Can I talk to you inside for a minute?"

A neighbor boy named Albert came running over with a friend and told me, "Don't go in there." He asked the fellow, "What you got in the paper?"

At first, the fellow wouldn't open it, but he changed his mind when he saw that Albert and his buddy were going to snatch it from him.

The fellow had a steel rod in the paper. He had been planning to beat me with it because he thought I'd actually hit the little white child.

Albert whistled and the other black boys started streaming down the block toward us.

Somebody yelled, "Get your knives out!"

The guy with the rod and his friend started running away from all those black boys with knives. Boy oh boy, 142nd Street was in a mess that day.

God was also with us that day. The neighbor boys were right to come to my defense because the man intended to beat me with the rod. I could have been severely injured, or even killed. But the fact remains that he was a white man being chased by black boys with weapons in hand. If he had summoned the police, all of us, including me, would have been rounded up and thrown into jail.

Somehow, I got the money to go see my mama in the hospital. Her eyes were sunken and tired looking. She tried to smile when I hugged her, but it didn't work. She wasn't doing too well at all.

Before we moved into our new place, Mama had taken sick at the other house. She was one of those people that stayed real quiet if things went wrong, but I guess after a while she couldn't keep her worries to herself. My aunt Tantee had come over one day and my mother told her that the baby hadn't moved in a few weeks. Baby? What baby? That's when I realized she was pregnant again.

So Tantee asked her what she was waiting for. "Why don't you go to the hospital?"

But Mama worried about leaving us, and probably trying to save a dime or two, decided to take castor oil instead. It caused a lot of rumbling in her stomach, but that is all. The baby still didn't move.

She got very sick and had to go to the hospital anyway. At the hospital, the doctors told her that the baby had been dead for quite a while. Now she was lying in front of me, and it was very clear that every word she spoke came with a great deal of effort.

When she came home, she was never the same. At her next appointment, they kept her. She lasted four months in the hospital. I went to see her after school twice a week.

Having the dead baby inside her had somehow affected her lungs. Up until then, Mama had been a very healthy person, but the baby had decayed in her body and all kinds of things went wrong. That very last baby killed her. She died in 1934 at the age of forty-five and was buried on her birthday, October 29th.

Yes, I cried for Mama when they put her in the ground. I felt sorry for her and the life which was filled with constant work. I felt sorry for me, but most of all, I felt sorry for the younger children. After all, I was nineteen years old. Some of them were still in grade school. I still needed Mama emotionally, but they needed her in a much different way. Poor little things. They could not understand where Mama had gone or that she was not coming back. It broke my heart to watch them weep.

Sorrow creeps up behind you sometimes and you can't see it coming. For a long time, I could be in the middle of talking or laughing, when all of a sudden, tears were streaming down my cheeks. I could be at work, snipping thread off a brand-new dress that had just come from the presser, when I would find myself wondering if Mama wanted me to help her cook when I got off. Almost at the same time, I would remember that I didn't have a mama no more and the tears welled up in my eyes. I had to blink them back because the last thing I needed was any kind of trouble on the job.

Mama had never been particularly jolly, and I can't remember her laughing much, but for some reason, after she died, I would see something that made me laugh and think how Mama would have found it funny as well. More tears. Sad events about someone we used to know or the death of a neighbor or casual acquaintance would upset me a great deal. Every itty bitty thing reminded me of Mama.

Long ago, it was believed that in times like that, it was better not to talk about the misfortune. We were taught not to speak of Mama's illness or the terrible silence that had descended on our home because of her absence. There is no way that this could have been good for Daddy or his children. Each one of us was a walking wound with thoughts and feelings all balled up in our heads and hearts.

Looking back, I think it would have been a lot healthier if Daddy and his children had talked about what happened to Mama. Or at least talked about her more than we did. Instead, we tried not to mention her too much so that nobody would start crying. We didn't know how to need each other. Instead, we just kept on working. Earning money was never a bad thing to do. You could count it. You could buy groceries with it. You could save it. It was tangible. Touchable. Not like feelings which were undependable and perhaps, dangerous.

We all pitched in and did all of the work that Mama used to do. As we got it all done, I found myself wondering how one person had managed to do it all. Poor Mama. I was honored to be able to see these things up close so that I never ever took her memory for granted. I faced all that work without complaint and remained undaunted as I knew she would have expected me to do.

That feeling of misery stayed with me for a long time.

While Mama was sick, the state had removed Daisy, Mary, and Tina because there was no mother to take care of them. Daddy worried about them constantly. "We have to get the tree (his pronunciation of the word *three*) little ones back," he said over and over again.

I wonder about that situation. Somewhere in big old New York City, there had to be households that were headed by a single male parent. Or, did the state remove minor children from every household when the mother died or was otherwise unable to care for them? It is a very strange part of our family story and I have wondered about it a great deal. Did Daisy, Mary, and Tina arrive at school looking unkempt a few times? Were they then questioned, and the fact that Mama had died had been determined to be the reason for an undone hair ribbon or a stained dress? Whatever the case, Daddy only shared what he figured was our business to know. Sitting around talking about the situation was not going to get the "tree little ones back," so, as always, action was required. Soul searching, analysis, and deep thinking were luxuries. Our family was missing three children and something had to be done.

So Daddy remarried. Our stepmother was called Mommy Dell, and as soon as she moved in, the state returned my little sisters because there was now a woman in the house all day to care for them. I guess the fact that I was nineteen and Omena was twenty didn't mean anything because we were always working.

Maybe working all the time kept the Potter girls out of the kind of trouble that so many parents feared. Although we didn't have too many pregnancies among the young people I associated with, I'm sure that my father worried about it just the same.

In our small Caribbean community, the parents was on the guy's back just like they was on the girl's back. They told us girls, "Keep your legs closed, dress down, drawers up." They told the boys, "Keep your pants buttoned up; I don't want your girlfriend's baby in here." They told us like it was. "Don't bring no babies in here."

These words were stated from between hard, definite lips in crisp, no-nonsense, don't-even-think-that-I'm-playing-with-you tones.

Many times while walking around Harlem, I would see a group of young girls (black and white) and at least one of them had her belly sticking out.

In our small community, if you saw five or six girls, nobody was pregnant.

None. That's right.

Generally in society at that time, there was more circumspect behavior among the teenagers. There was more respect for orders and the dictates of parents. In our community, we weren't even called teenagers. We were all called children until we got up in our late teens, early twenties.

There was one case where one girl was messed up and she and her mother didn't get along because she was pregnant. She applied for welfare and got it. The welfare caseworker found out she was eighteen years old and told her that she didn't have to put up with her mother's humiliation and tongue lashings over her condition.

"Oh, well you can get a place of your own," said the welfare worker.

That was the worst mistake they ever made, because if she could get a place of her own, all of the teenagers figured they could get away from home using that method as well.

Soon, many girls were living at home, pregnant and not getting along with their parents, then welfare gave them a place and furniture. In this way, welfare encouraged children to get away from home. All of a sudden, it was a big thing going on. And it was mostly in the black neighborhoods, not where it was all white.

I was twenty years old when I had my first date. My daughter, Cheryl, tells folk now that she "thinks it was the culture that kept Mommy from dating younger." She is right.

The tradition in the family coming from three previous generations or more in Anegada was that older children helped with younger siblings, the mother cooked and cleaned, while the father made the living for the family. So in our culture the daughters helped take care of the home and worried about boys much later.

The funny thing is that Daddy never talked to us about missing Anegada or the life there, or hinted that coming here was a disadvantage. He never gave us the impression that life here was a disappointment in any way and he never spoke of himself as an immigrant. He simply became an entrepreneur and he always made a way for his family. He never spoke of himself as anything other than an American.

When we grew up, my brothers and sisters would often share apartments to help each other get ahead financially. I think that this was another custom that followed Daddy and Mama here from Anegada. I think that visiting family members after the work week was also a tradition from the island. There was no real tourist trade on Anegada, so the people weren't going to some hotel to work on the weekends. Instead, they spent that time with family.

The way families made money was through fishing. The men would go fishing at three or four in the morning. The women would clean the fish. Small boats from the surrounding islands would pick up the fish and take it back for sale to the tourists. Ships couldn't get into Anegada when Daddy was a kid, because before the channel was built, they had difficulty navigating the reefs. Even now, boats to Anegada are chartered with great care because of the reefs. That's how both Mama and Daddy grew up, and how their parents grew up, and on back for a few generations. No one worked for other people. They worked as a community and as a family. The school on the island only went up to the eighth grade. So anyone who wanted to go further had to go to Tortola—a British island that governed Anegada.

So I helped with the little ones and did not seriously date.

At first, I went out with groups of people who were just friends. On Saturdays, we usually went to the movies. My father also allowed us to have company over. We had these new record players, and when our friends came over, there was lots of dancing, talking, and laughing. It would get loud. Every time Daddy thought it was too loud or they were staying too long, he'd walk through the apartment in his long drawers. He'd say, "I'm going to bed, I don't want to hear no noise." That meant it was time for our company to leave.

I wondered what Mama would have made of all the noise and dancing. Would she have approved or just went along with whatever my father thought was right? Probably the latter.

I loved going to the famous Savoy Ballroom. It had a huge dance floor and the club itself took up an entire city block from 140th to 141st Street in Harlem. There were two bands each night and they took turns playing tunes that kept the crowd dancing. Monday was a treat for the girls. We got in free and the boys still had to pay. Boy, those floors were slippery. The Lindy Hop dance was in then, and it was done much different than the way they show it now. When the boy threw you out and spun you around, you had to come back to the right hand. It was bigger and faster. There was also more movement. When they started throwing girls over their heads, I didn't go for that. No way. I was afraid they was gonna drop me. I was never for too much roughness because I know I'm not that big.

Nobody had too much money back in those days. If you went to the movies or something, you paid your own way. One fellow and I agreed in the beginning that we would go to the Apollo one night. He paid his way and I paid for myself. So we went and saw Moms Mabley. She was a comedian who dressed up in old lady clothes and looked like she had no teeth. To look at her, you would think she was not too smart. The look was deceiving. She was very smart and she told very funny jokes about life that were right on the mark. Everybody loved Moms Mabley. She told one joke that ended with the line, "Men are like buses. There is always another one coming along."

I should have taken that joke to heart and believed in it. Maybe I wouldn't have been so quick to get so serious about the first guy I fell in love with.

I had dropped out of Textile High School and started working in the factories at age seventeen, making six dollars a week. Even though it was a small salary, I was single and just helping out at home, so it went a long way. Three big rolls were five cents and a large loaf of bread was ten cents. Butter was sixteen cents a pound. On Friday, the fishman came around singing, "Bring down your dishpan, here comes your fishman." For fifteen cents, your dishpan was filled with fish. Potatoes was one cent a pound. Kale was three cents a pound.

I always wanted to have a bank account. When I saved up five dollars, I went to Carver's bank and opened up an account. You would have thought it was five hundred dollars the way I was hanging on to my bank book. I felt like I was as rich as Rockefeller.

I talked about my new bank book a lot, and when I reached twelve dollars, I was ecstatic. Everybody in the house had to hear about it. Big mistake. Daddy borrowed twelve dollars from me and I asked him for weeks to pay me back. I approached him one too many times.

"Daddy, I want my money back."

His chest swelled up. He blew air in and out of his cheeks before looking me and up down in disdain. "Who do you think you are to demand money from me?"

I said nothing.

"Eh, girl? Answer me. You think you grown enough to live on your own? You think you grown enough that you don't need this house?"

"No."

"Well, what then?"

"You asked me to loan you the money, not give it away to you."

This was way more impertinence than he could stand. He pointed a long brown finger toward the front door.

"Pack your things and get out of my house. Right now."

"To go where?"

"Wherever grown women go who don't need their father's house anymore, that's where."

Then I knew how Oswald must have felt when Daddy told him that he couldn't stay at home anymore.

Since I didn't have anywhere to lay my head, the best thing for me to do was get a sleep-in job. That was exactly like it sounded. You lived in the house where you worked as a maid and nanny. You pocketed a small salary, but at least you had a room and food to eat.

There were plenty of employment agencies that specialized in sleep-in jobs. The way it worked was that you signed up and paid them a fee to help you find work. If you didn't have the money to get a job, they would not help you.

I went to a company on 135th Street and told the owner that I had no money to pay. I promised to give him the fee as soon as I got paid. I guess he looked at me and saw my pitiful desperation because he thought about it for only a minute before saying okay.

He made some calls and got me a job right away

"Do you have the carfare to get there?"

"Yes," I lied.

I felt too sad and ashamed to say no. Wasn't Daddy worried about where I might have gone?

The man nodded and told me that I'd be working for a Mrs. Mendleshon. The job paid thirty dollars a month. I thanked him and headed uptown to the Mendleshon residence on 224th Street and Van Cortland Park. It was a very long walk. When I rang the bell, I was tired, hungry, and upset.

The first thing Mrs. Mendleshon wanted to know was what took me so long to get there. At the time, I thought she was being unreasonable, but she probably thought I'd been fooling around somewhere before getting on a bus.

Before I could answer, she ushered me inside and told me that my job was a mother's helper. She also told me that she could pay me only twenty-five dollars a month and not thirty as the agency had promised. I said okay and she took me to my room which was off the kitchen. Suddenly she looked at my empty hands.

"Where is your suitcase?"

"I don't have a bag."

"Is this your first employment?"

"Yes."

She gave me a housedress and some slippers that someone else had left behind before introducing me to her five-year-old son, David. After that, she showed me the house, which was big and nice. Everything went fine for the next two weeks.

Then one evening, I finished all my duties and went to bed. About two hours later, I heard a man's voice outside my bedroom door. He was calling my name. It was Mr. Mendleshon. I did not answer. He stayed there so long calling me that Mrs. Mendleshon eventually heard him, came downstairs, and asked what he was doing. He said he came downstairs to get a drink of water. She replied, "You can drink water upstairs."

When I heard her voice, I opened my door and asked him to please stop calling me because I was afraid. He got real nasty, called me a liar, and told me to get out.

Mrs. Mendleshon said, "She can't leave now. It's dark outside. We'll get in trouble."

I guess since it was the middle of the night, she thought that I could get badly hurt and they would get the blame for it.

So the next day she paid me $13.50 and gave me five cents carfare to get home. I was nervous and shaking inside. Once again, God had stepped in and saved me. The woman could just have easily gone back up those stairs and pretended not to hear the sexual assault that was surely coming.

In those days, the body of a black woman was fair game. If that man had even gone so far as to rape me, there wouldn't have been anything done about it. That was always the problem working in folks' houses whether you were a sleep-in maid or just came in to clean every day. Some women had to submit to the urges of the husband. In other places, it was an uncle, an adult son, or even a guest of the family. Black women for the most part didn't even bother to report unlawful touching, sexual assault, or rape. What would have been the point? The court system was set up to protect the men and make the woman look like a tramp. Plus, there was nowhere a black woman could go where it was different. From what I heard, the homes of the wealthy in New York City were a treat compared to what was happening to the maids in states below Washington, DC. Down there in the Deep South, if a black woman refused, she could find herself accused of stealing from the family, which meant automatic jail time. It was terrible!

I always thank God that Daddy and Mama settled in the North. God knows what me and my sisters would have gone through in one of those Southern states.

Traumatized and with nowhere else to go, I showed up at Daddy's door. He didn't mention the twelve dollars that he owed me. He didn't ask where I'd been for two weeks. He didn't welcome me home. Nothing. He simply let me in and walked away. I felt so unwanted. I can't describe the hurt to this day.

I went back to the factory.

There were plenty of factories. You could always get a job in the factory. If you were at one place and couldn't get along, you'd just go back outside and try another company. Every time I got a garment, I would look at it and think, *Let me see, what would Mama do?* and then I did the same thing. I was very well liked because my work was fast and it was good. I made all kinds of clothing. Plus, I knew how to work as an operator, a finisher (the person who sews on all of the collars, buttons, and does the hem after a garment is finished), and a trimmer, who takes the garment from the presser and cuts all of the loose strings away. Pressers did not do anything else except iron the garments. Once the trimmer was through, then someone came in and swept up the area. The boss came in after that and all of the garments were put in plastic bags and hung in specific places according to which store they were going to. Back in those days, everyone had one specific job and stuck to it. One person was not expected to do every step that it takes to make a garment.

I had a problem with one boss. Every time this manager started talking, he would spit. My father advised me to hold a handkerchief up to my face when it happened. That handkerchief got me fired. I know that the boss felt insulted, but I couldn't have him spitting on me. How did I know what kind of disease he had?

When the manager told me I was fired, I said, "I don't care. I been in better places than this."

I went just a couple of doors away and there was another operating job. Factories are also seasonal places. Sometimes you get to stay, but most of the time you go from one place to another. The only way you could run out of work to do was if you only knew how to do one thing. Like if you only knew how to make dresses, for instance. There was no guarantee that you could work steady. I didn't do just one thing. I could make any garment, including children's coats. When, for some reason, most of the factories were closed for sewing work, I did crocheting. Once, I worked in a place that was preparing for the Christmas rush and all I did was decorate crocheted skirts for the dolls. I had liked crocheting since I was a child and decorated some of our clothing even way back then. After the doll rush was over, I got a chance to work in another factory that focused on hats. The hats were already made, but I had to add designs to the brims or fine stitching around the edges. I got most of the skills, such as sewing dresses, from my mother's teaching. The rest I learned on the jobs. Most of the factories would show you exactly what they wanted. I learned fast and did exactly as they asked.

Socially, I was still going out with groups of friends and did not take any guy seriously until I went out with Darryl Richardson. Everybody called him Rip. He was a Jamaican man, born November 11, 1911, which made him four years older than I was.

I met Rip through my brothers. He was a driver for a Pepsi truck and younger boys hung out at stores where he did a lot of business. My teenage brothers hung out at a stationery store where he delivered soda. They became good friends and he started hanging around my house. He was always coming over to see my brothers. After a while, we started going out.

Then one day, he said to me, "Gee, you so nice. I'd like to marry you. You want to get married?

"What? I'm not so interested in marriage cuz nothing out here for nobody. Times are hard and nobody got no money."

"Well, looka here, Miss Ida. I'm going to give you my ring and this will be our engagement ring."

He took a ring off his finger and put it on mine and I started wearing it.

Right around this time, all hell broke loose in Harlem and it caused me to worry a lot anytime I didn't know where Rip or my brothers were. I feared that they had been beaten or arrested.

What happened was that tensions caused by employment and police brutality boiled over on March 19, 1935 when police arrested a young Puerto Rican boy who'd been caught stealing a pocketknife from a store. In an attempt to avoid crowds that had gathered, the police whisked the boy out a rear entrance and rumors spread that police were going to beat him. More rumors asserted that the boy had been killed, although police had circulated pictures of the lad, showing him very much alive.

Mayor Fiorello La Guardia pleaded for calm and patience, but his words fell on deaf ears. Rioting started, and by the end of the next day, March 20, 1935, three African Americans had been killed, sixty were injured, and seventy-five people, mostly black, had been arrested.

It was a terrible time, and I was nervous anytime Rip or one of my brothers could not be found.

Our engagement went on for about a year before I took the ring off, saying I wasn't into it. Then I thought about it some more. I loved him. He seemed nice, he was always working, he was very well mannered. I decided to take a chance on love and told him that I changed my mind. So Rip gave me back the so-called engagement ring. It was September 1936 when we got "engaged."

"Why can't we get together for real?" he asked me one night as he kissed my cheeks.

I said okay.

Yes, I knew that sex before marriage was wrong. That had been drilled into my head. But this was not head. I was thinking with my heart. We got together for real and then one more time after that. Soon I started feeling strange, like I wanted to throw up. I went to a doctor and he said, "You're three months pregnant."

What? Oh no!

For the next few hours, I wondered what day we would get married, what on earth Rip and I were going to do with a baby, where we would find a place to live, and how we were going to get it all done before my father found out what I had done. Those questions were at the forefront of my mind.

When I told Rip, he said, "I don't have any money right now."

"Well, we don't have to have some big fancy wedding. Let's just go on down to city hall and get married, then have a little gathering back at my house."

He shifted from one foot to the other. "I don't want to do it like that."

"What is wrong, Rip?"

"Let me think about it all, Ida. Can I do that?"

"Okay, Rip, but we don't have a lot of time."

I thought that something was wrong but I couldn't figure out what it was. It occurred to me that he might just be nervous about the whole thing. One day he is a free delivery truck driver. The next he is a married man with a child on the way? I figured that maybe he just needed a few weeks to get used to the huge change that was coming in his life.

Weeks went by and I was becoming both suspicious and impatient. I had heard about girls getting left with nothing but a big stomach to show for their foolishness, but Rip couldn't be trying to do that to me, could he? After all, he was a good friend of my brothers'. He knew my father. He was always around our house. I wasn't some chippy that he had just rolled around with for giggles.

Another month went by. Rip and I were not on good terms. I was nervous and suspicious. His cheer seemed forced.

Round about November I got a letter. It had probably come for me the day before because I had seen a white envelope in the foyer. Now, I had taken a closer look and seen my name. Since it was Thanksgiving Day, I continued on helping out my family with the cooking and all. Dinner was festive. Everybody was in a decent mood and the room smelled good because we had been cooking all day.

After dinner was over, we all sat down and had some lemonade. Then I went and read my letter. It was like somebody poured a ton of ice on me. The person who sent me the letter had been one of my classmates in seventh grade. Her name was Ina May Swain, and her letter said, "You are having a baby from my husband."

What? It can't be!

I was so shocked that my throat closed up. I couldn't even swallow. My Thanksgiving holiday was ruined.

When Rip came by the next day, I flung the letter at him. "You are married?"

"No. I'm not married. This is a lie. This lady just wants to hurt your feelings."

"Do you know her?"

"Yes. I used to be her boyfriend. We talked about getting married. Then she didn't want to. Then she did again. I got tired and stopped asking her. I don't know when was the last time I saw her. I don't know why she would do this unless it is because she is still angry with me."

Satisfied, I stayed in the relationship. Time was running out. I would soon start to show. One evening, I cornered him.

"Rip. My house is too crowded. You need to find another place to stay."

I expected him to bring up marriage right then. What on earth was he waiting for?

All of a sudden, I was afraid to bring up the word *marriage* again. I guess deep down inside, I was scared that he would walk away and leave me.

Daddy figured everything out. I was sick a lot, and since I'm so thin, he would have noticed the tiniest bump that appeared around my waist.

If he was disappointed in me, he didn't say so. Daddy didn't make me feel bad in any way about my predicament. He wasn't the type of man to waste time or energy on a situation that he could not fix. As far as he was concerned, I had made a very hard bed for myself to lie in and nothing he said or did would make a bit of difference, but I was still grateful to him for not shaming me. He turned out to be right on all counts. There was no need for him to punish me. I was about to be punished severely enough for what I had done.

Like many people who were trying to make ends meet, Rip's mother was renting rooms to lodgers, so we moved into one of them. She worked as a charwoman for Western Union, cleaning up the doors and outside. African Americans were given the worst jobs available, especially if they were from another country.

After a while, Rip's mother started complaining that we wasn't paying no rent, so I thought, *Oh Lawd, I gone from the frying pan to the fire.* The bickering continued. By May I had no choice but to go back to my father's house *again*. It was time for me to have my baby.

His mother had always said that Rip lived with her and slept on the sofa. I later found out that Rip was so sneaky, it was ridiculous. He actually didn't live at his mother's house at all; he had a place of his own uptown. She had to know that I was not aware of whatever bachelor place he had. Did she tell him that he was doing me wrong and needed to come clean? Or, did she dislike me so much that no matter what he did to me, it was alright with her? I never approached her with those questions because I had too much pride. I didn't want her to think I was begging for something. Or worse, give her a chance to really insult me.

My house was just plain overcrowded. Mommy Dell and Daddy now had a nine-month-old boy. After the situation with Rip's mother didn't work out, I realized that he wasn't going to marry me and probably never had planned to go through with our engagement. If he really wanted to marry me, he would have. Why let me go back home to have the baby?

After the baby was born, I decided to just go out on my own and continue working. Daisy (who didn't get married until much later when Daddy had passed away) was still at home. I could bring the baby to her every morning and pick it up at night.

Anyway, I did the best that I could. At first, I shared an apartment with one of my friends. Actually, it was my stepmother's friend and it didn't work out.

Under the best of circumstances, roommate situations do not work out. At first, I was relieved to get the place. It seemed like just what I needed. The woman wasn't a stranger and I was tired of trying to figure out my life on my own. A friend seemed like just the ticket. It would have helped if we had known each for a while and already decided that we liked each other. Instead, I had a fretting child, worries that kept me awake staring at the ceiling, and although I tried to be cheerful, it was probably crystal clear that I was always worried about something. Maybe she wanted someone to share the place who would be fun, gossipy, and a confidante. Since I was none of those things, she complained to Mommy Dell that she had changed her mind. I needed to leave her place, and sooner rather than later.

I didn't know what to do when the roommate situation fell apart. I said well, I'll have to make it on my own. I got myself in this stupid mess, I'm gonna have to get myself out. But Rip's mother said, "Well you can leave the baby here because Danny (her husband) is here all day."

If I had had the time to be sad because Rip was not acting loving at all or being protective of me or his child, I probably would have been tearing my hair out. As it was, keeping a roof over my head and food in my mouth took over just about everything else in my mind.

I still loved Rip but I wasn't stupid enough not to realize what had happened. All I could do was take care of myself and hope that he changed his mind and married me down the road. I really couldn't handle any other kind of thoughts. It was just too scary.

When I got pregnant, I decided I might as well have a healthy baby, so I started with the orange juice and a whole lot of stuff Mama used to give us for breakfast, like oatmeal and prunes.

Donald was born in 1937, and he moved around so fast, he fell off the bed at three months while trying to crawl.

My second child, Charles, was born in 1939, and at that point, I still had hope that Rip would get himself together and make us a real family. I had been with Rip for two years and some small part of me wanted to get back together for the sake of our boys.

By the time Charles was six months old, he was even more

active than Donald had been. I had some strong babies. One day, Charles was on the bed sleeping near the window because it was warm. The rooming houses didn't have things like window screens. I stepped out of the room and accidentally closed the door behind me. Since I had a slam lock on it, there was no way for me to get back in. I left the building screaming and ran down to Lenox Avenue. God was good to me. Right on the corner was a locksmith. I was so upset, I couldn't even talk straight. I ran in there just babbling my baby is gonna fall out the window, my baby is gonna fall out the window over and over again. The locksmith came back to the building with me. When he got to my room and saw it was a slam lock, he picked out a special key and turned it in the lock. The door opened and we went in. Charles was still asleep. He had slept through the entire drama. Thank God!

If there were any tiny parts of me that still subconsciously wanted Rip, they were about to be smashed to bits.

It turned out that Rip really did have a wife. In fact, their first child was born the same time as my Donald. I thought of all those lies he had told so smoothly and so clearly. Years later, he and his wife ended up having seven or eight children together after we broke up. If there was one thing in my life that I've always regretted, it is believing Rip when he told me that the woman's letter was full of lies.

The thing about Rip that just made me confused was that I didn't just run into his arms the very first time he showed interest in me. I had known him for a long time just as a friend of the family who was often in my home. We took it slow, or I took it slow. I didn't chase him or try to rush him to get married when he gave me the engagement ring. He was always nice, polite, and respectful before I got pregnant. How could he treat me this way? I guess it doesn't matter how long you wait and try to get to know a person. There was just nothing I could think of that would explain how he was ignoring me and my problems most of the time. When I found out that he was indeed married, I was just sick to my stomach. There is no other way to put it. Just sick.

Playing his wife dirty was bad enough, but how could he give me an engagement ring when he knew that he wasn't free to marry me?

I had to go through chronic homelessness and fear without being able to take the time to grieve the loss (because this new Rip was someone I neither knew nor understood) of the man I loved. I was sad about the pain and embarrassment that he had caused me. I was sad for his wife and knew that she would never ever believe that I had not known Rip was married when I first agreed to go out with him. To add to the sadness, I felt like a very foolish young woman. I remembered telling him when I first found out that I was pregnant with Donald that we could go to city hall and have a get-together at my house afterward. Worse, I now realized that I should have hardened my heart as soon as he started running away from the suggestion.

I wished that I could ease my pain and the heartache that his wife had to be feeling, because by now, she surely knew about Charles, that Rip not only had one son outside the marriage but two.

I felt even worse when I found out that both of my brothers had known that Rip was married and didn't warn me. What kind of code did they live by where this could possibly be okay? Did it mean that male friendship came before blood? They hadn't said a thing. After it was all over, I said to them, "I'm your sister. He was just your friend. And you knew all of this? How could you not tell me?" Their answer was, "Rip told us not to tell you."

I am over a hundred years old now and I've seen a lot and lived a lot. I understand more about people and their motivations. But even though I forgave my brothers long ago, I will never understand their silence.

Rip wasn't giving me any money, so I had to move from place to place. I kept getting kicked out of apartments because I couldn't keep up with the rent. The mess was getting too thick. I started to understand why people commit suicide and take their children with them. I had to talk myself out of it by reminding myself that there was no way for me to get through the gates of heaven if I had taken my own life. The Bible is very clear on the subject of suicide.

Then, there was the issue of murder. I had to look in the mirror and say that word out loud. My boys had a right to live.

God sent Donald and Charles to me for safekeeping and I was thinking like a coward.

After dismissing the plan to kill myself, I got the wild idea that my boys were going to turn out just like their father and that I should just walk away, leave them, and go off someplace by myself. I decided that that was crazy too. I had to pull myself together.

At this point, Omena was living with my mother's sister, Aunt Tantee. Omena suggested that since I was having such a hard time, I should stay with her and Aunt Tantee. I felt relieved and headed with her to Aunt Tantee's house. It didn't go like we'd planned. After a week, Aunt Tantee said that I could stay at her house during the day while she was at work but that I'd have to find somewhere else to go at night.

Instead, I put the boys back in the carriage and went to the police precinct on 136th Street. I told them that I had no place to stay and two small children. They gave me carfare and sent me to a place on Sixth Street and Sixth Avenue.

That is how I ended up in a homeless shelter with my two boys. We stayed there almost a year. I applied for welfare (technically the name was Aid to Dependent Children). The investigator tried to make me go back to Rip because he had a job, even though he had a terrible gambling problem and owed his boss a lot of money. But since Rip and I were never married, they could not force him to take me and the boys to the room he was renting. Finally, welfare gave me the much needed funds to get on my feet. Now, don't get me wrong, I didn't like being on welfare. If you have a birthday and somebody gives you some money or something, you got to report that. If somebody gives you a gift just as a favor, you got to report that. It was hard. But they did help me get an apartment and that was what I needed most. I've never been afraid of hard work and I don't believe that anyone owes me a living or free money. But I did need a home for me and my children.

When we left the shelter, Donald was three and Charles was almost a year old. I paid $22 a month rent for the new apartment and my light bill was sixty-seven cents. All of this happened in 1940.

Then World War II started and jobs began to open up. So, I found a job and got off welfare. That was a big mistake. There were no childcare centers. You had to just find someone, anyone, to keep your child, and it was at your own risk. There was one babysitter that I took them to for a while. I took them and their food to her every day, but when I went to pick them up, most of the time they either had sore throats or diarrhea. Many children were getting hurt and neglected in these unregulated places.

I took Donald back to Rip's mother and let Daisy keep Charles. She was home all the time because she was not a real outgoing person. I did this for about eight or nine months and then Abyssinian Baptist Church started taking care of kids, so I took Charles there. It cost ten dollars a week and it gave Daisy a break. It felt safe. By then he was almost three. Donald was still staying with Rip's mother and father.

When Abyssinian stopped keeping kids, a new group formed in the neighborhood. The deal was they would watch your kid for half your paycheck. They were unregulated and could do as they pleased. They actually demanded to see your paycheck before they signed you up just to make sure they were truly getting half. Now, I was making twenty-nine dollars a week. Half of that would have left me with hardly nothing to support three people, so I had to rely on neighbors to keep my children. This meant that I was upset all day on the job because I didn't know how they were being treated. Many other women were in my position. We tried to stick with whoever seemed to be nice to the children, but you just never knew.

I took Rip to court for child support and the judge ordered him to give me five dollars a week. That was $2.50 per week per child. I was supposed to go to the police precinct every week to pick it up. Since I had to work and find a place to leave the children, I figured that I would collect it every three weeks and then it would be a whopping fifteen dollars. I did not know that my plan was not workable. No one told me that if I didn't show up every single week, the money was automatically returned to the father. So when I finally went to get it, the money was gone. Rip had it back in his pocket. I decided not to go back to the courts and fight again. Somehow, me and my children would find a way to make do with what we had.

I decided that all men were no good . . . just a bunch of users. I went on working in the factory and taking care of my children the best way I knew how. In the factories, I got a couple of raises and I even made it up to a position called Floor Lady. Then I made it up to Assistant because I had caught on to everything so quickly, like measuring the strings which go around each garment. With each promotion came a few extra coins, and I needed every single one of them. I began to feel good.

Then I got the heartbreaking news that Estelle, one of my childhood playmates, had died. I remembered the time when she forgot her keys and I went into her house through the window to get them. Like me, Estelle was only in her early thirties. What on earth had she died from? It took me a while to get the story, and when I learned what happened, it just made me sadder. She had just had a baby and had taken a bath. Her grandmother warned her not to go sitting out in the damp air to be with the baby's father. Anyway, she came down with tuberculosis and died. She didn't last no time. The baby's father and his family took custody of her child. I ran into the baby's father many years later. He said that the baby had grown up just fine. That made me happy.

Even though he hadn't given me one dollar while I was in the shelter or tried to give back the fifteen dollars that the police had returned to him, Rip soon surfaced when I had a small change of fortune.

When Rip found out that I was out of the shelter and had my own place, he came back. He looked around the new apartment and gave me a big smile. "Gee, this is nice," he said. "Can I get a key?"

A slow burn started from the tip of my toes and quickly flared into my stomach and on up to my head.

Did this man think I was a total idiot, or did he think that he was so irresistible that I would be willing to sleep with him again and get a third child? No matter what he thought, I was furious. I turned around and faced him nose to nose.

I can't tell anyone what I said to him. Let's just say that it wasn't at all ladylike and definitely not very nice.

Rip and I were over.

CHAPTER 5

MOMMY DELL

Mommy Dell was a Negro with a Southern background that had its roots in slavery. Originally from Charleston, South Carolina, she was a very tall (much taller than Daddy) brown-skinned woman with a terrific smile. People always remembered Mommy Dell's smile. Her first name was really Adele, but back then young people did not simply call adults by their first name. Something had to go in front of it as a sign of respect. So once Daddy married her, she immediately became Mommy Dell to me and my siblings.

Daddy met Mommy Dell after he had lost all of the businesses and got license to stand on 139th Street to sell fruits and vegetables from a pushcart. He met Mommy Dell when she became one of his pushcart customers. She had never been married or had children and was living with relatives (cousins, I think) in New York City. Daddy and Mommy Dell became friends, and after my mother passed away, they just got closer. Daddy didn't just up and marry her right away, so it was two and a half to three years before they got married. Finally they got married, and almost immediately she got pregnant. They had a baby named Joseph, but we called him Bootsy. I had had my baby, Donald, along around the same time. After my father got himself together, he got another apartment and I moved in with him and Mommy Dell until I could move out with my baby. So at one point, Donald and Bootsy were babies in the apartment together.

Mommy Dell was a very useful person. In other words, she was no slacker. She worked hard and liked nice things. Even though she was twenty years younger than Daddy, the two got along real good. I thought Mommy Dell was nice, but sometimes I felt sorry for her. Because she was pretty and so much younger, Daddy seemed to keep a tight leash (like some older husbands tend to do) on her. He didn't want her to go anywhere without him.

The only thing that I didn't like about Mommy Dell was the extreme measures she took to get a bit of privacy in the house for her, my father, and Bootsy. She actually had a couple of guys move some of the heavy furniture around so that it created a barrier between her little family and the rest of us.

The only thing Mommy Dell ever did that was really wrong was take some money out of Daddy's stash and then lie about it. She was young, pretty, and maybe not used to living such a bare bones lifestyle. The desire for an inexpensive string of pearls made her filch a few dollars to buy them. Scared, she hid them and told Daddy that she had seen me go into his tin bank. Of course, I denied it but he believed his wife. She and I were on bad terms for a few weeks over that.

On the other hand, Adele did introduce us to Southern cooking, which we were not used to at all. Our diet had always been Caribbean based and it took some time for us to get used to the new flavors. I learned to love fried chicken and barbecued ribs even though we had always stewed or baked our meat. Even though I liked some of her dishes, I did not adopt her recipes to serve my own children. Stewed, baked, or broiled was the name of the game in my home. It is a lot healthier.

Occasionally, some of Mommy Dell's relatives would come up to visit her from down South. They were nice and fun, but I don't think they were used to being around Caribbean people, and a lot of our ways may have seemed strange to them. When Bootsy was about three years old, she sent him to Charleston with a pack of them so that he could get accustomed to his Southern heritage. Daddy insisted that Bootsy had to be educated in New York City, so he came back in time to start first grade.

After about four years, the asthma which had plagued Daddy for most of his life became a whole lot worse. He started getting sicker and sicker. After a while, he could no longer stand on a street corner in all types of weather and sell fruits and vegetables from a pushcart. He and Mommy Dell began to argue over money, Bootsy, and God only knows what else. She went to stay with her New York City cousins for a while and then they got back together. When they broke up again, it was for good and she moved down to Charleston.

Bootsy stayed in New York with Daddy until he was about sixteen years old. That's when he got arrested for marijuana possession. Well, Daddy would never put up with that kind of behavior. When Bootsy got out of jail, he went down South to live with Mommy Dell, and I only saw him once after that. It was in the 1980s when we got word that Mommy Dell was dying.

Apparently, she started getting seizures, and after taking medication for some time, the medicine wouldn't work anymore. I went down South to see her. After I got back, we heard that she had passed away.

Bootsy did not keep in touch with us after his mother died and I don't know what became of him.

CHAPTER 6

DADDY

Daddy was born in 1886, one of sixteen children. That wasn't all that unusual back then because there was no birth control. Only three of the children (Daddy, Adena, who was called Dinah, and Cecily) emigrated to America. The other thirteen never even came for a visit.

Daddy died in 1963 at the age of seventy-seven. At the time of his death, he was living on the top floor of a six-story apartment building which did not have an elevator. His asthma had become chronic over the years and there was simply no way that he could climb the stairs, so he rarely went outside. We had to bring everything he needed to his apartment.

He must have been extremely lonely, but there was not a whole lot any of us could do about it on a daily basis. We were all too busy just trying to keep our families afloat. Worse than the loneliness was probably the lack of activity which burdened him. He had always been a man with a money-making plan, and now his health was much too bad for him to work. My brother told me that he was getting some type of financial assistance, but I can't remember what government agency was furnishing it.

Sometimes, Daddy would tie a string around a pail and slowly let it down the side of the building. One of my brothers would put supplies (bread, juice, sandwich meat, toilet paper, and other small things) in the pail and Daddy would pull it back up the building and carefully bring it back through his window. When no one else was available, he would pay Cheryl to run up and down the stairs doing errands for him. He was always so sick from the ongoing asthma attacks that everyone believed it was that disease which would ultimately cost him his life. We were all wrong. Daddy had a heart attack in 1963 and died shortly after arriving at Harlem Hospital. When he died, I refused to let Laura and Cheryl attend the funeral because they had been so upset after attending their father's services years before.

Daddy's sister, Adena, had done very well for herself in America. She owned a private taxi company that serviced Harlem with a small fleet of cars. She purchased Harlem brownstones when they were dirt cheap. When Cheryl grew up, she purchased them from Adena's only surviving child, Ralph. He charged Cheryl $150,000 for the best one, but there were squatters living there and she had to pay each one of them off so that they would leave. Cheryl truly has Daddy's entrepreneurial spirit. She renovated that building at a cost of $350,000, which she had to get loans from the bank to do. Then she sold the building for a million dollars, paid off the loans, and pocketed the difference.

Daddy's sister, Cecily, went to Santo Domingo (and therefore spoke Spanish) before coming to America. In New York, she did domestic work for a rich woman who had some connection to a candy fortune. It is said that the woman practiced mixing chocolate for candy in the same pan that she soaked her feet in. According to the tale, Aunt Cecily spent a lot of time warning guests and other visitors not to eat any candy out of the pan.

Cheryl really enjoyed the real estate business. Outside of Adena's property, her first purchase was an apartment building that had nine six-room apartments. She and a doctor went in on it, chipping in something like $10,000 apiece. I didn't like the sound of that even though he sounded like a trustworthy man and seemed very nice. It was just that Daddy had had such bad luck with partners that I wanted Cheryl to stay away from those kinds of arrangements. She felt the same way. Having a partner made her so uncomfortable that the two of them ended up selling the building and that was the end of that.

Neither Mama nor Daddy ever returned to Anegada.

THE STARS

While traveling by train on my vacation

sitting by the window.

I happened to look up

so many stars.

I started to wonder

if the skies above

were as crowded as earth below.

CHAPTER 7

FINDING MY WAY

Then the Lord *God said, "It is not good*
for the man to be alone. I will make
him a helper suitable for him."
—GENESIS 2:18

I was totally disillusioned with men and had no interest in getting into a new relationship. In fact, I decided not to ever be bothered with any more men. I started to feel that they all were a bunch of liars because I used to hear my brothers trying to jive some girl. I also decided not to waste any more time being furious with Rip or feeling sorry for myself. Yes, I had made a hard bed for myself and I couldn't yet see my way clear to peace, but his wife was the one with the problem, and I should consider myself lucky that I had not ended up legally married to him so that he could cheat on me and have babies with some other woman. I had two small boys to raise and I needed every drop of my energy to get that done right. There was no way that I could stay furious and be focused at the same time. When he and I broke up, I was finally established in my own place and had a reliable factory job. It was a time for looking forward, not backward.

I stayed to myself a lot and went to the library when I could to take out books of poems and whatever I could find about American history and also the story of black people. Reading was a way to educate myself since I had never gone to college, and it also helped keep myself sane. There I was, not even thirty years old, and my life was already mapped out as far as I could see. It consisted of backbreaking factory work, child raising, housework, and church. That was it and there was nothing in my line of vision that indicated it would ever change. Sure, the boys would grow up and marry. So then I'd be alone in the house which would still need cleaning, and working at the factory to pay bills that still needed paying, and on Sundays, I would go to church and ask God to give me strength to do it all again the next day.

Reading gave me hope that things could (I didn't know how) turn out different for me. It also kept my spirits up and hope alive in my heart, because a lot of what I read made me wonder how people went through such trials and tribulations without losing their mind. I began to feel fortunate that I was existing in this time and space instead of being alive during slavery or the terrible years when the Jim Crow laws were created to keep black folks scared and on guard.

In other words, reading made me see just how much worse my life could be, and I was grateful to God for sparing me those horrendous experiences.

It was after World War II when my life changed again. I was somewhere one day and this fella kept looking at me and looking at me. My first thought was, *What you lookin' at?*

It wasn't that I was a mean woman. It's just that I didn't like men leering at me. I thought it was fresh, and to smile at him would have meant encouraging possible bad behavior. So I frowned and turned away. Figuring that was the end of it, I started thinking about something else.

He came over and said, "Excuse me, I don't mean to be staring at you, but you look so much like someone I knew in the service."

I said, "I have a brother in the Army. His name is Oscar."

"Oscar Potter?"

"That's him," I confirmed.

"Well, ain't that something. My name is Lawrence Keeling. I was Oscar's corporal."

We went on from there. He entertained me by telling me a lot about my brother's ups and downs. It was clear that he respected Oscar and that made me feel good.

At first, we would just go out for a drink or two. Then he wanted to get serious. I was fearful. I liked him a lot, but it seemed like men sometimes want to tear a woman down so that they can build themselves up. No. I felt free. I didn't want anyone telling me what I could and couldn't do. Where I could and couldn't go. I had thanked the Lord for granting me some peace of mind.

He asked, "Would you like to spend some time with me?"

That meant sex and a whole lot of promises that he wouldn't keep.

"No way. I don't want to hear that stuff anymore."

"We could get married," he added.

I was no longer a naïve twenty-year-old girl and I was not about to get trapped up in a new mess. This man was definitely rubbing me the wrong way.

"I heard that mess before too."

He just laughed that day and shrugged it off. We kept on being friends. I realized that if we started dating, Charles and Donald would be in a sense dating him too. In other words, if he was hanging around our apartment, my children would be stuck with whatever I was doing and not be able to express their feelings about it. Then, he probably would want to spend more and more time with me, and I barely had enough time for the boys as it was. They might start to feel like they were being replaced or something. If I started spending all my free time with him, he was bound to get full of himself and think that I desperately needed a man. Then he would start taking me through changes. He would just have to give me more time to get to know him. Maybe this was nothing but a fly-by-night friendship, and if that was the case, my kids never needed to know he existed.

Lawrence Keeling was nothing if not persistent. One night we were at a bar and having a terrific time. He said, "There's this church right down the street. Won't you please marry me?"

I decided to take another chance on love.

That was June 22, 1946. The church was at 1202 West 144th Street near Lenox Avenue, around the corner from the bar we were sitting in. It was 12:30 a.m. when we got the pastor out of his bed to marry us.

I still had my apartment, so afterward we talked things out over there.

I got pregnant pretty fast. I was three months pregnant when I had my first miscarriage and six months pregnant when I had the second. Both were boys. I think the miscarriages happened because I did a lot of standing on my feet. I needed to be quiet. I am a very little person and it was hard for me because I had to go to work and stuff like that. It took a lot of physical effort to stay employed during those pregnancies, but we needed the money.

Then in 1949, my Laura came along and her delivery was very hard for me. I was terrified that something was going to go wrong and she would die before I even got a chance to hold her. She was my first girl.

Cheryl came along in 1951, and that was a nice, easy birth. After Cheryl's birth, I decided that I was finished. There would be no more children for me.

Lawrence was good to me, plus he worked hard at the post office and paid the bills. I had only two concerns. First of all, he knew that I had two sons when he married me. Yet, once we were all living together, he didn't try to hide his disinterest in Donald and Charles. In fact, he wanted them to go live with relatives. I said, "No, I'm not putting my children out for you."

The other problem was that he liked the bottle a little too much. It is annoying when someone is tipsy and you are not.

A lot of new buildings were going up in our area. One of them opened up on 159th Street. It was called the Colonial Houses. Lawrence went right away and got five rooms for us, and it was a happy day for me when we moved in. It was a really beautiful place.

Lawrence worked hard in the post office, and at first he was a good husband even though he liked to drink.

I later found out why my husband drank so much.

His father, James Keeling, and his mother, Genevieve, had six children: Nathaniel, Lil, Naomi, Leon, Lawrence (my husband), and Harold. James was brown skinned. Genevieve was light skinned, fair enough to pass for white.

Their first two children were very light, sandy haired and gray eyed. The second two were red haired with hazel eyes. The last two were darker than the other four.

James decided that Genevieve must be having sex outside the marriage or his last two children wouldn't be so dark. He killed her with a hatchet. Their children came home from the movies and she was dead. There was blood everywhere. My husband was a teen when his mom was murdered. His aunt had the place cleaned up and let the kids stay there in the same apartment. She paid the rent and bought their food. The second eldest boy, Leon, took on the role of father to his five siblings. James Keeling died in a mental institution.

Although my husband, Lawrence, did not witness the slaughter of his mother, he did come home to the blood splattered home after a fun time at the movies. I guess a memory of that would make anyone drink. He must have felt very scared for a very long time after that day. These days, all of the Keeling children would have probably been sent to therapy to work out their feelings about what had happened to their mother.

All I could do when he drank heavily was pray for him. I prayed a lot.

Lawrence and I had a few good years, but then he started messing up the money and I wasn't making enough to cover his mistakes. After struggling financially for a time because of his irresponsible behavior, I threw in the towel. I told him, "Look, I can't deal with this." And that was it.

We separated in 1953, but he used to come by and see the children. Once, when he came for a visit, he asked if we could get back together. He said, "I'm gon' do better."

I told him I didn't want to hear all that stuff. I had been through too much in my life. I told him I'd had enough mess with men. They all say they gon' do better and then they get in and better is forgotten. Enough. Time marches on."

Alone once again, the Colonial Apartments became too expensive for me. So me and my four children moved into a one-room place until I could find us somewhere else to live.

We stayed in that one room for quite a while at my friend Margaret's house. Donald spent much of his time at his grandmother's place. The girls and I slept in the one bed while Charles slept on a chair with his feet on the bed. Then I got lucky.

In June of 1955, I moved into a fairly new housing project called the St. Nicholas Houses. It had only been up and running for about a year. In fact, there was still work being done on the grounds. The housing project was eleven buildings, with fourteen stories in each building and eight apartments per floor. On the fifth floor where we lived, there were twenty-one children. I moved in when I was forty years old and lived there until I was seventy-three years old. A total of thirty-three years.

We were lucky to get an apartment in the projects.

With the arrival of the 1950s, blacks were still struggling to achieve their American dreams in Harlem, but oppressively high rents were a source of constant irritation and despair. Rent strikes were called to draw attention to the larcenous prices imposed on renters and move landlords to rectify long-standing problems with rats, roaches, and providing heat during the winter. For Harlem's black residents, the discrepancies in housing availability, quality, and pricing were problems that had existed since the early twentieth century. African Americans paid higher rents in Harlem, in part as a result of landlords outside of Harlem refusing to rent to blacks. The insult of higher rents was compounded when blacks were confronted with paying the inflated prices for accommodations that were substandard and decaying. The general pattern was that the worse the accommodations, the higher the rents.

Life for most struggling people in New York was quite hard at the start of the twentieth century. For struggling people of color, including immigrants of color, the historically toxic racial climate in the United States compounded the material burdens of building an existence that offered some degree of comfort, dignity, and happiness.

For African Americans and immigrants of color, living conditions in New York at the start of the twentieth century could leave one breathless. Just over two and a half million people, roughly two-thirds of the city's overall population of just under three and a half million, lived in eighty thousand tenements. Not all tenements were clusters of overcrowded humanity and incubators of disease, but there were enough to be a persisting problem of concern for urban reformers.

Federally sponsored housing projects were built to accommodate the increased numbers of blacks who streamed in from the South to fill the numerous open vacancies in the armaments industry. In Detroit, the city whose name became synonymous with the title "Arsenal of Democracy," the Sojourner Truth housing project was located in a part of town where, according to the rationale of officials in the federal government, there should have been little resistance from white residents in nearby neighborhoods. After a long period when the Sojourner Truth occupancies remained vacant, six black families finally moved in. It took over one thousand city and state police officers with the backing of well over a thousand members of the Michigan National Guard to see to the protection of the six families who, after all, were only seeking shelter.

When we moved into the projects, Laura was about to turn six and Cheryl was four. I put Laura in school and registered them both in the children's center at the St. Nicholas Houses. So that was a break there when it came to child care.

My father had taught us not to get what you don't need and not to go after anything you can't afford. My sisters and I followed those lessons as adults, and I taught them to my children. They had to save a portion of any money they received, no matter how they got it. They were not allowed to throw away the portion that they were allowed to spend. The girls had to spend most of it on something that they needed and not always on something silly and useless that they wanted. One very important lesson that they had to learn was how to wait. It is usually the case that when young people get a dime in their hands, they want to spend it right away without thinking, without preparing, without even giving a thought to the value of the dime and how lucky they were to get it. No matter what the girls decided to spend their loose change on, I made them wait at least a day and think about the purchase. No impulsive spending. That kind of behavior leads to problems when they're grown up.

So, through careful money management, I was able to pay my bills, including the $56 per month rent.

By that time, my boys were big, in their late teens, and I encouraged them to go out on their own. I wasn't willing to take care of any man, whether it was my son or not. It was also important for my children to learn to stand on their own two feet. By then, Charles had gotten mixed up with some girl, so he moved out, but he came by often. I was surprised that Charles even listened to me and moved out because Charles had always been such a mama's boy.

I cautioned all my children about their choices, just as my father had done to us. He didn't talk much, but what he said went right to your head. He was a firm believer in that old saying that "if you make your bed hard, you got to lay in it."

After Lawrence and I broke up, the post office let him go. I didn't know that they were going to do that just because I had complained to them about his not bringing home his paycheck. I was shocked. But he did it to himself. It turns out that he had been drinking on the job as well. They had been pretending not to know because he was a very good worker, but finding out that he also had problems at home forced them to do something. I didn't know all of that until much later. All I knew was that Lawrence was running a tab at the liquor store even though he knew that our rent wasn't paid. I wasn't able to shoulder the financial burden by myself, plus I didn't know what he was doing with the money that he had stopped bringing home. Soon, I had an eviction notice and I went to the post office to see if they could send his pay directly to me since he was being irresponsible. I had no idea that they would get rid of him, but I can't let anybody run all over me. It was a terrible situation and it was time for him to find another place to live.

Don't get me wrong. I did not arrive at that decision lightly. I knew what it was to be the only breadwinner with two kids looking at me for something to eat three times a day. I knew what it was to be separated from the father of my children and having no one to bounce ideas off or consult about anything when I really needed someone to talk to. I knew what it would feel like to have my girls asking when Daddy was coming home. But with all that drinking, I was getting little to no emotional support anyway.

When I think about all that I had gone through up until that point, I feel like screaming.

My husband moved around a lot after that, from his sisters' to his brothers' homes.

The doctor had been telling Lawrence to stop drinking for years, but he didn't listen. He died of a heart attack at age forty-two.

The funeral was a nightmare and it was with this that I made one of my biggest mistakes as a parent. I took our two girls to their father's funeral. They had never been to one before and they became very upset. Afterward, it took a lot of work for me to help them get over it all. I think the biggest problem was that no matter how hard things had ever gotten for me, they had never seen me shed a tear. I, as the widow, sat up front on the first bench. My girls sat right behind me. When that organ music swelled up, I broke down. My girls started whimpering at first, but after a while it all became too much. Cheryl actually climbed over the bench to get to me instead of simply going into the aisle and walking.

Lawrence and I had never divorced and I never remarried.

MOTHER'S DAY BLUES

I love you mother
said John Jr.
forgetting his chore.
His cap went on and
off to the playground swing
leaving mother the wood to bring.
I love you mother
said her daughter.
Sure, after breakfast
I'll do my chores.
I promise you.
Before she could do her best
telephone rang.
When she put the receiver down
off she went in a flash.
Leaving the kitchen in an
awful mess.
I shall return soon said her husband
John Sr.
to prepare dinner
then we will go to a movie.

That will be nice said his wife.

it will make my day.

Hours later when the phone rang

I'm stuck in a card game

her husband said.

Well, replied his wife

you've ruined my day.

CHAPTER 8

SINGLE MOTHERHOOD

Children are a heritage from the Lord,
offspring a reward from him.

—PSALM 127:3

There I was with four kids to finish raising, two from a broken engagement and two from a marriage that had not worked. Donald and Charles were already in their late teens with serious girlfriends and rarely lived at home. When they were younger, I let them both become Boy Scouts to keep them out of the streets and give them some more values to live by. I also used to take them to the armory where they could run and exercise in a safe place. I was determined to keep my sons out of trouble and far away from street life. After the breakup with their father, I didn't want them anywhere near him. He was a plain liar from start to finish. I knew that he owed a lot of gambling debts, and I was fearful about what else he might be involved in that could get my sons into trouble. But now they were young men who didn't need me as much. They knew right from wrong. So when I found out that they were spending time with Rip, I didn't try to stop them.

My focus was on my two little girls. Laura was now nine and Cheryl seven.

I did not wonder what would have happened if I had insisted that Rip marry me before we became intimate. I refused to consider how my life would have been different if I had not believed Rip when he told me that he was not married. Regrets in the form of shoulda, coulda, woulda don't do a body any good. In fact, sitting around thinking like that can either paralyze you to the point where you can't move forward at all or just plain drive you crazy. I never saw either of my parents look back in regret and whine about what did or did not turn out right. I worked very hard to follow their habit of looking and moving forward. Up till this point, my ability to keep on keeping on no matter what happened.came directly from their examples.

I'm sure that Laura and Cheryl did not have everything they wanted, but neither has memories of going to bed hungry, sitting in the dark because I didn't pay the light bill, or coming home to find our belongings on the street because I didn't or couldn't pay the rent.

I made sure that my girls lived in peace. Our apartment was free of the arguing, physical violence, and strife that was part of the lives of so many people that we knew in the projects. But I could not control what they saw or heard when they stepped outside the cozy environment that I created for them.

When I moved into the St. Nicholas Houses, it was a great relief to find that they had doors on the closets. I had lived in many tenements that didn't have doors. I made drapes, kept the house clean, and every Saturday I washed all the windows. I learned how to play the numbers, which was like today's lottery games except that it was run privately by individuals and there were no taxes taken out of the money. I rarely won, but if I did, I'd buy furniture or clothing or stuff for the house like clocks and towels.

Very often there were emergency situations in the projects, and police or an ambulance were needed to help someone or to restore peace. There used to be a joke that if you wanted them to respond to your emergency, the best thing to do was to call and say that you were a white person. One nice chocolate brown lady had some friends who took that seriously. She had fallen and someone called the ambulance. It seemed like the ambulance was taking a very long time to get there, so some of the guys called the precinct and said, "There is a white lady on the ground out here and all of these guys are just standing there looking." The police and the ambulance arrived in seconds.

I always had at least two jobs. When I worked at the factory, I also worked at the Horn and Hardart restaurant. After I had taken a typing course and found work at the Hebrew Congregation, I also worked at Sons and Daughters of Israel. Sometimes I would be so tired. When I would get in the bed, it seemed like every side I laid on was exhausted. By the time I finished all four sides, the alarm clock would go off and it was time to get up and do it all over again.

There was a period where I had two jobs but money was still so tight that I figured out a way to get a third. It was just for a few hours on the weekend and I didn't plan to keep it more than six months. So one night I took Laura and Cheryl to Omena's house.

Now, Omena's next-door neighbor was a beautiful single woman named Ann who had two boys of her own and a no-account adult brother who also stayed in her apartment. Well, Ann was a gorgeous party thrower who was always dressed up and never seen in the wintertime without a fur coat on, probably given to her by a boyfriend. She was very pretty and was considered quite a babe. She used to like to have parties, and there was always noise and laughter coming from her apartment. Anyway, the brother fell asleep with a cigarette in his hand and it started burning the sofa cushion that he was sleeping on. Ann's place filled with smoke and the smell seeped into Omena's place. She opened her front door to a hallway clogged with smoke and a screaming Ann who had stepped out and was now being restrained by firemen. My kids remember Omena pushing them hard in their sleep and then dragging them out of bed and to the fire escape.

Both of Ann's little boys died in her apartment that night. Her brother somehow got out alive.

When I got off the train and was coming down the street, I could see the big, charred black hole on the fourth floor of Omena's building. Some woman who had witnessed the tragedy came up to me and said, "Isn't that sad that both of them died?"

I was sick.

I started running until I reached Omena who was standing outside with my two precious girls. I have never been so glad to see them.

I hope that my daughters never knew when my fingers ached or my neck and back hurt from working hard. I never wanted them worrying about me simply because I was doing what a mother is supposed to do. I could not afford to fall apart, because

My father, Osbourne.

Standing on a Harlem street.
I'm twenty-six in this picture.

Me at the park with family. Left to right: Bunny, Bessie,
Herman on Bessie's lap, me, Daisy, Nollas with Lydia on his lap.

I'm pictured here with my coworkers at Union of American Hebrew Congregations. I'm second from the right.

A Christmas long ago.
On the left: me, Charles, and Donald.

To the right:
Donald and me.

My son Donald as a young boy.

My son Charles as a young boy.

My sons, Donald and Charles, with their father's parents, Matilda and Danny (center, behind the boys).

My siblings at a dinner party. Clockwise from the front left side:
my sister Daisy with her husband, Fitzherman Dickson;
my sister Mary with her husband, Bill Beal; my brother Oscar
with his friend Enash; my sister Quentin with an unknown friend.

My siblings and me at a birthday party. Front row, from left to
right (sitting on the floor): brother-in-law Roy, Mary's husband;
sister Daisy; Daisy's lifetime friend Connie. Second row, left to
right, starting from second from the left (standing and seated):
family friend Ann; sister Mary; me; sister Quentin; brother-in-law
Howard, Quentin's husband; sister Omena. Third row, from the
right (standing): brother Oscar, niece Rosalind, niece Barbara.

Donald in his dress clothes.

Charles in his leather jacket.

My husband, Lawrence
Keeling, and me.

My husband, Lawrence Keeling,
with our baby Laura.

Lawrence, me, and baby Laura.

Friend Amelia and me after dropping off Laura and
Cheryl at America Fresh Air Camp in 1958.

A photo Donald sent to me. He was in training in the US Navy.

Charles (middle) at the bar with friends. He was overseas.

Charles with Mikki, the professional dancer he fell in love with in Watertown. They were leaving Laura's wedding.

My niece Celeste's birthday party. Cheryl is on the far left, and
Laura is middle right with the pointy birthday hat. Front row,
from left to right: Cheryl, Celeste, Phyllis, Angie. Second row:
Herman, Deborah, a neighborhood friend, Laura, Lydia,
a neighborhood friend. Back: a neighborhood friend.

My daughters as young girls.
Cheryl (age four) is on the left and
Laura (age six) is on the right.

Donald and June,
his first and only wife.

My girls in 1962. From left to right: Cheryl, Laura, and me.

My son Charles in Okinawa, 1964.

Me in the 1970s.

Oswald (left) was a chef as a merchant seaman for United Fruitlines.

Me at a camp in Liberty, New York (Catskills).

A picture of me in the kitchen.

Me in the 1980s.

My daughter Cheryl and me in the 1970s.

A party. From left to right: me, my cousin Ralph,
and my sister Omena.

From left to right: my sister Mary, my sister Omena,
my son Charles, me, and my sister Daisy.

My seventy-first birthday party.
From left to right: Laura, me, and Cheryl.

My eighty-first birthday at Tavern on the Green. My friend
Pecolia and me, plus my grandchildren Lloyd and Hayward.

Me in my nineties.

I won the bronze at the World Athletic Veteran Games
in Buffalo, New York, in 1995. I was eighty years old.

Running the 800 at
the World Athletic
Veteran Games.

Cheryl and me.

Photo: Norman Jean Roy / Art+Commerce

if I went down the tubes, I would take my two smart and beautiful girls with me. I could not afford to pay attention to the neighbors who felt that I thought my kids were better than theirs simply because I wanted the best for them.

Sometimes I needed help either financially or just someone to listen while I worked out a problem. I usually turned to my brother, Oswald. He was the brother that was always there for his sisters. Whatever you had to do, you could count on him. Oswald used to shine shoes at Mr. Rose's every chance he got. He saved over fifty dollars. Mama wanted to put it in the bank for him, but Daddy took it.

Oswald stayed with me and my daughters whenever he was on leave from 1956 to 1960, but after four years, I wanted him to find his own place. Even though he helped me out a lot by giving me money and always bought us nice things, my girls were growing up, so I needed my space. Daisy and I helped him to find an apartment that he enjoyed until he started having kidney trouble. After working in the merchant marine for thirty-eight years, he was relieved of his duties in 1972 for medical reasons. He was sick on and off after that, in and out of hospitals, and passed away in 1988. I still don't think that Daddy should have kicked Oswald out of the house when he was only seventeen years old. Daddy should have been proud of him for getting his own cart and earning his own living. I think Oswald had guts.

Omena and Daisy lived together and they watched Laura and Cheryl while I was working, sometimes as many as three jobs.

When neither one of them could babysit, I left the girls with Miss Washington, our neighbor. In exchange for her help, I took care of Miss Washington's little baby when she had things that she needed to do.

I took the girls to church every Sunday, but I would not take them early in the morning. They got up very early to go to school all week and I worked all week. My children and I needed our Sunday mornings for relaxation and reading the paper or talking. We went to church around 1:30. I made sure that they were raised in the Methodist church because both my parents had been Methodists. Salem Methodist had been my childhood home church, so that is where we went even though there was a Baptist church close by which had afternoon and evening services. For a time, both girls took dancing lessons. They didn't get a lot of sweets and rarely ate fried food. On Sundays, I usually made pot roast. On other days, we mostly had lamb stew, liver and grits, fish and grits, or boiled spareribs. The menu was pretty much what Mama had served me and my siblings when we were growing up. The girls were both good scholars and made excellent grades in school. In fact, Laura ended up getting skipped a grade.

The St. Nicholas Houses began to change when drugs took over in the 1960s and 70s. Of course, there had always been drug activity, particularly when heroin was all the rage, but overnight it seemed like there were junkies everywhere. All lined up against one of the walls where my children could not help but see them as they walked to and from school. Worse, drug dealers began to live in the buildings. During the crack epidemic of the 1980s, it became a downright vicious place to live. I could only hope that the madness would not find its way into my home.

Once the girls got into high school and I had more time for myself, I went back to school. I loved math and I loved learning about office procedures. I also learned new machines. I catch on pretty quickly. I took some night classes in math, keypunching, and working the collating machines. Then I was able to get out of the factories and get some office work. I felt like a big shot.

I had lived through the Great Depression so I knew how to get through hard times. The Depression taught people how to stand on their own two feet and make do with what they got. Back then, everybody was broke.

As the girls were growing up, I was kind of strict for one simple reason: I had to work and they needed to obey the rules that I laid down in order for everything to run smoothly. As soon as Laura turned ten, I tried to give her a key to get in and out, but she was scared and didn't want one. Instead, I gave it to Miss Washington, our neighbor. Laura would come home from school and pick up the key from her and go in the apartment and they could start with their homework. I tried to get home as early as I could. They had their chores to do, shopping, and washing some of their clothes. They also had to clean the apartment, except for my room; they were not allowed to go into my room. That went well. Sometimes my girls spent weekends at the home of their father's brother, Leon Keeling. We visited often because I wanted to stay in touch with the Keeling family. I also liked to take Laura and Cheryl with me to visit my own aunts and uncles who were still alive.

I used my free time to be with my girls so that they would know they were important to me.

When we couldn't think of anything else to do, we took the ferry to Staten Island. We had hot dogs and soda on the ferry, and once we got off, we walked around and then had some dessert. Then we'd come home and eat our beans and rice and whatever else I had cooked and that would be the end of the day. We never had big money, but I made do. My daughters say that "Growing up, we knew that we were the most important part of Mommy's life. We had a rich life and never felt that we missed anything."

When the girls were growing up, they got along pretty good because they were only a year and ten months apart in age and had the same ideas. As time moved on and they split up and went to different colleges, started traveling and got different friends, everything seemed to change. Little jealousies about this and that started popping up. Only one thing remained the same: the dedication to family. They respected each other's talents and abilities, and although the closeness seemed to go away, they came together when it came to kinfolk. When something came up related to family that needed to be discussed, they would do that, but the friendship was never as strong once they got older.

My neighbors believed that I thought I was better than everybody else. It wasn't that. I just wanted my girls to have a real chance in life, so I kept my distance. When I came out of the building, sometimes they'd yell, "Hey, Big Money." They called me that because me and my girls always looked nice. When we came out of the building, we were headed somewhere. We didn't just hang around outside the projects. My children and I always had a destination. My neighbors didn't know that I had nothing, although they should have since we were all living in low-income housing together. Then they started saying that I was raising my kids like they were white just because they had dance lessons and went to a free sleepaway camp every summer.

My elder daughter, Laura, was picked on in school because she was dressed nice and didn't behave in a rowdy fashion. She kept to herself all the time. She preferred reading books to playing outside. The other kids told her that she thought she was better than them. They didn't know that Laura was simply shy.

The family is supposed to stick together if they can help each other. But if I had to do it all over again, I would have said no to some of my family's requests. At least a few times. I was the sister who would never say no and everyone knew it. It made me vulnerable.

I had always wanted a nice fat bank account, money put aside in case real hard times came back, but there was always a setback. In fact, every time I tried to start a bank account, something happened in my family. My relatives knew that I believed in saving, so the thinking probably went, "Oh, Ida probably got some money. Let's go to her." It seemed like every time I saved up at least two hundred dollars, somebody was in need and I had to part with it to help the person out of a bad situation.

All my brothers had pretty good jobs by this point. My older brother, Oswald, was a seaman. He worked for the United Fruit Line. The middle one, Nollas, worked at the post office. All my brothers had been in the service and so had both my sons. One of my nieces and her husband even retired from the Air Force as lieutenant colonels. We were hardworking people with big ideas and little pay. All I had done was the factories, Horn and Hardart restaurant, and a few low paying clerical jobs that I worked at for some time after I came out of the factories.

I never made nothing over minimum wage all my life. But I kept up with my bills. I used to get compliments from the gas company, the light company, and the insurance company because as soon as I got the bills, I paid them. I didn't want to deal with late payment fees and other things that dribble away your money. Paying interest and things like that was a bad idea. You ended up paying twice as much as you originally owed. I paid the whole bill right away. It helped clear my mind which was messed up enough.

Both of my girls were always in the classes for gifted children. In fact, they were featured as outstanding children in a booklet that used to go around the district. When they got older, I didn't have to tell them to get jobs. They really wanted to work. In fact, Cheryl once got a summer job by lying about her age. You had to be at least fourteen to get working papers in New York City. She was younger than that. Both my girls were happy when they finally turned fourteen and they were able to work legally. Both got jobs. The jobs were part-time and paid only around thirty-eight dollars. I told them they had to get their books and stuff out of that money.

As my girls got into their teens, they went to parties but had to be back at a certain hour. They were very good at following my rules.

Sometimes I would get ahead just a little bit and someone would ruin it. That got on my nerves. One time, I managed to save money to get a little washing machine. It was cheap, nothing fancy, but in the projects every little thing is a big deal. My neighbors saw it being delivered to my apartment, and the next thing I knew, one of them asked if she could come over and wash some of her things. "I'll bring a bottle," she said. "We'll hang out."

It was common in those projects for people to start hanging out in your house and using up all your resources so that they could save their own. From what I had observed, they usually brought something—food, drink—at first. Then they simply started showing up and consuming what you had. By that time, it would be hard to complain about it because the assumption would be that a close friendship either had developed or was in the works.

My answer was firm and final. "No. Don't even start it."

Then Charles came by and wanted to wash some stuff. I said that he could, but I noticed a buckle on a pair of pants that he wanted to wash. I told him not to put the buckle part in the machine. I left the kitchen where the machine was hooked up. I wasn't gone long before I heard a popping sound. He had not listened to me and the machine broke. That was the end of that.

Then the boys started getting into trouble. Charles wound up in the youth house and I had to go down and get him out. Folks told me that he and his friends partied on the roof a lot and took girls up there. Something was bound to go wrong and it did. It turns out that Betty was one of those girls up there on the roof with Charles. He got Betty in trouble (which was what they called pregnant back then) and she was only thirteen years old. He was almost seventeen. The truant officer was after the girl's mother because she had been out of school for thirty-four days. The mother tried to tell him that the girl had been coming to my house. I said no way. The two of them had been getting together on her grandmother's roof. There was no way I would have allowed any sexual activity in my house.

Betty had the baby at age fourteen. She had nothing to offer any guy, no home of her own, and she was at a spiteful age and an age that can be very stubborn. At fourteen years old, a girl goes through chemical changes and body changes. I was that age myself and know what goes on. Charles had nothing to offer Betty either. They were just two teenagers who had gotten themselves in a real mess. The problem was that everyone in her family decided that I had to be the one to fix what was definitely unfixable. What was I supposed to do? There was no putting that genie back in the bottle.

Once Betty had her baby girl, her mother tried to pawn the whole situation off on me, but I was not having it. The last thing I needed was Charles, an infant, and an underage girl bringing people in and out of my house while I was out trying to make a living for me, Laura, and Cheryl.

But the situation grew desperate, so I ended up letting them stay. It was a terrible situation because Betty came from a good home. I tried to keep her from getting pregnant again after the first child was born by telling her to do something with her life because "Charles doesn't want anything." It was a situation that should not have happened. She wasn't some tragic kid out of the projects. In fact, she didn't even grow up in the projects. She lived with her mother and grandmother nearby in a very nice apartment building. Mamie, the grandmother, raised Betty on 143rd and Seventh Avenue. Betty was a very uppity, light skinned girl whose mother and grandmother wanted her to have the best.

Mamie walked around with what she thought were high-class mannerisms, but she didn't take no crap off no man and would throw them out if they didn't act right. Although Mamie was tough talking, she was very loving with Betty, who was a pretty girl. Mamie had her in Catholic school. The uniform was how kids distinguished themselves from the public school kids. Betty was fun and had a great laugh. Her youngest child, Juanita, laughs just like her.

Betty grew up an only child, but when she was a teenager, her mother Gloria gave birth to two more children from some guy. Their names were Bobby and Brenda.

When Betty got pregnant with Denise, Gloria threw her out. I eventually let her move into my house. When Howard was born, the baby was brought to my house. What could I do in this situation? I couldn't see those babies end up in the street. But watching a child try to be a mother was hard to do. One time, Betty was scolding two-year-old Denise for peeing in her pants, and Cheryl got very angry because Denise was just a baby. But Betty simply had no mothering capacity and was doing the best she could. Whatever she thought she might have had got used up because there were so many babies. They were all at my house, and after Juanita was born, she and Charles moved out again and got an apartment. They used to come on the weekend to see me.

Then something strange started to happen. Betty showed up one time without Juanita and said, "She is at my friend's house in Queens." It happened two more times and then I demanded to know what was going on.

The answer deeply saddened me. When Juanita was fifteen months old, a family in Queens adopted her because Betty was no longer able to take care of so many kids. She didn't want to give any of them up, so she struck an agreement with the adopted parents. Juanita grew up thinking that the adopted parents were her real parents and that Betty was her aunt. Betty just couldn't stand to completely let go. Charles went along with it, telling Betty, "I ain't no good. I ain't got no job."

Cheryl was still having trouble with the parenting style of Betty and Charles. Once Charles hit little Howard at the dinner table. Cheryl ran away from the meal and into another room. Charles went behind her and said, "Listen, lil sis, I don't want him to grow up like me having nothing and not finishing school. I want him to learn to act right."

Eventually, the situation just became too much for me and my girls.

Gloria had to let Betty move back in because she was under eighteen. Charles couldn't stay with me and he couldn't stay at Betty's home. One night, he went to his grandmother's (Rip's mom) house. She was not home, so he climbed up onto her fire escape which faced the street and tried to get in through the window. Someone saw him and assumed that he was a burglar trying to break in. The police were called and that is how Charles ended up in the youth house until the whole mess was straightened out.

It was clear that neither Charles or Betty were going to change. Both of them were going to keep on doing what they were doing. It was all about drama and what they thought was passion. In reality, they were just creating a deeper and deeper mess.

When it came time to go to college, my girls both won scholarships. I had told them all their lives that I could not afford college tuition, and without scholarship money, they wouldn't be able to go to college. I wasn't even able to collect any weekly money from the military pension that I thought their father had. I received one check during all those years and it was for a very small amount. When I asked for more, I was told that Lawrence Keeling didn't have enough credits or whatever they called it. I just let it go and didn't fight. This was happening to many families. Some people were wondering if it was a terrible scheme that had been planned before the boys were even called into service for World War II. I didn't spend too much time thinking about it. I just moved on and made do.

Throughout the years, I told Laura and Cheryl, "Stick to your school work. Understand that you have to go to school every single day. Make sure that you always do your homework on time, keep a good attitude, and don't be afraid to ask the teacher questions no matter how mean you think she is. She knows what she is there for." I didn't have no trouble with my girls and they both won college scholarships.

Laura's first scholarship was for such a small amount that she took it and went to Bronx Community College, which was a two-year school, instead of going to a four-year college.

She graduated from the two-year college and then went on to New York University where she earned her bachelor's and master's degrees.

After Cheryl finished college, she applied for money in 1974 from the Model Cities Program (one of the only programs in the nation that gave money for graduate and professional study at that time) and received three thousand dollars which she used to pay for law school.

After everyone was grown and gone, I felt that the burden

was off. I had done my job to the best of my ability. It was time for me to pursue my own interests and leave my girls alone to live their lives.

I felt free. I felt better. I finally went back to school.

It wasn't college because I didn't even have a real high school diploma. Instead, I found workshops, programs, and some vocational schools that worked around my still hectic schedule. In 1969, when Cheryl was eighteen and Laura twenty, I earned a certificate in Record Keeping, Office Procedures, and Switchboard Operations. Then I did a ten-week program in typing that was being given by the State of New York Department of Civil Service. In addition to that, I did my civic duty and earned a certificate of service from the New York City Housing Authority for devoted service to the St. Nicholas Houses' Tenant Patrol. I did another ten-week program in bookkeeping, and finally it was enough. I was out of the factories for good and working full-time at Harlem Hospital in the records department.

I could get dressed up every morning in a skirt and blouse or a pretty dress and heels and go to work looking stylish. I was flying and happy. I felt like a big shot.

DRUG HORROR

Horror is the name of the drug game used

by weaklings, chickens, punks and chumps

eyes closed, knees sagging, dirty, greasy
    and grimy.

Think you're looking cool

standing there like a fool.

Smelling bad

face so sad.

Digging, scratching, make

no mistake,

there is a

monkey on your back.

You say you're doing fine peeping

through those out of focus eyes

trying to communicate with a

blown mind.

To yourself please kind

and a new life

you will find.

D.R.U.G. stood for

Developing your mind strengthen

your body.

Reaching out to help another younger

than yourself.

Uplift yourself.

You'll have no sorrow.

Get together again at the

drug called horror and you'll

have a better tomorrow.

CHAPTER 9

CIVIL RIGHTS
AND WRONGS

Anyone who claims to be in the light but hates
a brother or sister is still in the darkness.

—1 JOHN 2:9

I was sixteen, my sister Omena was seventeen, and Oswald was fifteen when we started paying attention to the plight of Negroes (the term *African American* was way in the future) in America. We got to thinking about all of that kind of stuff when Marcus Garvey and his organization, the United Negro Improvement Association, came along. White residents feared the influx of blacks into Harlem, but with the dawn of the 1920s, Harlem became identified with black culture, black life, and the black intelligentsia.

Aptly referred to as the Harlem Renaissance, black artists and intellectuals were part of the larger social mix that highlighted

African Americans' dynamic ability to succeed in spite of Jim Crow. Among some writers of the Harlem Renaissance, the optimism that had accompanied America's April 2, 1917 entry into World War I to help make the world safe for democracy gave way to a more jaded perspective that confronted American racism on the written page. One person who, though not an artist, nevertheless articulated the determination of blacks to shake off the shackles of white supremacy, was Marcus Garvey.

Born in Jamaica in 1887, Garvey, like many Caribbean blacks, sought his fortunes in America. He arrived in New York in 1916 after long being aware of the challenges confronting his African American brethren. As the founder and leader of a Black Nationalist movement embodied in the United Negro Improvement Association, Garvey directly challenged American racism and black lethargy. Speaking from Liberty Hall, a Harlem building he purchased in 1919, Garvey appealed to black pride, stressed the necessity of black economic empowerment, and spurned all hope for an integrated America. It is possible that my father heard Garvey speak and that would certainly have increased his desire to be his own man and added to his burning ambition. Garvey's rousing messages added their own element of electrifying presence to the dynamism of the cultural leaders of the Harlem Renaissance.

We were entranced. We loved hearing his speeches on 125th Street. Garvey believed that "a people without the knowledge of their past history, origin, and culture is like a tree without roots." Hearing him speak was when I learned that what I thought I knew about the African continent was completely wrong. I wondered why.

Long before the cries of "Black is beautiful" that came from the politics of the 1970s, Garvey said, "The Black skin is not a badge of shame, but rather a glorious symbol of national greatness." Contrary to what the press reported about him, he was not trying to get every single Negro in America to board his ship and move to Africa. In fact, he thought that was a very bad idea and said, "I have no desire to take all black people back to Africa; there are blacks who are no good here and will likewise be no good there." What he wanted black people to do was realize that the greatest slavery is mental slavery. Those are the shackles that he urged people to recognize and cast away.

When he lifted his arms and shouted, "Up you mighty race, accomplish what you will," there was applause from the crowd.

All I can say is that people like Marcus Garvey helped to drag some black people out of the crazy self-hatred that existed during the 1930s. Back then, many black folks didn't want to be called black or hear anything about Africa being our home. That is because in school we were told that Africa was a jungle filled with cannibals. Teachers never told us of the diamond and gold mines, the zinc, copper, rubber, and oil, or that most of the time Africa was feeding the rest of the world. Neither did they tell us of the rape of Africa by other countries. Another thing is that we were not encouraged to visit the library or to learn of our beginnings as kings and queens of the richest continent in the world.

Garvey was a very exciting speaker, and listening to him, I had no doubt that black people were capable of incredible accomplishments, many more than I had ever heard of. The message that Garvey put forth excited Omena and Oswald so much that they got the courage to get up on their soapboxes in public one day to speak about the problems that plagued black folk.

Marcus Garvey and his group were fine with me, but I was

more taken with the flamboyant man who called himself Sufi
Abdul Hamid. He was the leader of a group called the Oriental
Oxidental Scientifical Philosophical Society. To me, he was well
learned and a great orator. His speeches were both fiery and educational. Eventually, he led a small movement aimed at protesting
the hiring practices in Harlem. Most of the stores would not hire
black people even though they had set up shop in the black community and had predominately black customers who made them
rich. Suffi spoke out against that all the time. I enjoyed him very
much and Omena, Oswald, and I were members of his society
for a time.

Franklin Roosevelt was very popular with the black folks
of Harlem as well. I voted for him in 1932 when he ran against
Herbert Hoover and became President of the United States. It
seems to me that our faith in him was well placed. He became the
first president to appoint an African American as a federal judge
and to promote a black man to the rank of brigadier general in the
Army. But, most important, I have since heard that he was brave
enough to speak up and call lynching what it was. He came out
and said that it was "a vile form of collective murder." Black folks
used to vote Republican before Mr. Franklin Roosevelt appeared.
After he came on the scene, most black people became Democrats.

Racism was very real back in those days and you could be
walking down the street minding your own business and suddenly find yourself in a situation which could easily become life
threatening. One day, Omena and I went down in the subway,
headed for Chambers Street where there were a lot of factories. Omena was looking for work in downtown Manhattan.
Chambers Street and Canal Street always had "Help Wanted"

signs out. You could always get some type of work sewing any-thing from bras to coats. Well, when me and my big sister got off the subway, a white man took his elbow and deliberately slammed into her. I cursed at him and then he came hanging over me. I saw some black folks standing around and this gave me the courage to ask him, "Why you hit my sister?" He said, "I can't stand you niggers." I told him, "Go back to your cave." He reached up like he was going to hit me. One of the black men grabbed his arm and twisted it all around. Then the police came. One of them asked me what the problem was. I told him that the man was a coward who just started picking on women. I looked at the man again. "Here's a man. Why don't you make believe he don't have a badge and pick on him?" The man answered, "Oh, you must be crazy." I answered, "Crazy like a fox, just like you." My sister and I walked away and went about our business.

Omena got a job. She worked a while. She didn't like factory work so she went on back home and that was it.

That could have gone very badly for me and my sister. Our parents taught us to simply ignore white folks in order to avoid trouble. But sometimes you can't ignore ignorance. I've seen a lot of racism. We used to live right across the street from a tailor, and on the wall outside his shop were the words "Ball Playing Prohibited." One day, a boy was playing with a ball, throwing and catching it against the wall. Here comes this policeman. He grabbed the boy. The boy's mother saw it from the window and came running down the stairs, screaming, "That's my son. He don't know what prohibited mean. It's just a wall and a boy with a ball." The policeman told her, "You are interfering with police business," and shot the mother. Then the father, who was coming home from work, went over there to see what was going on. He tried to help his wife who was bleeding. The policeman said, "Don't put your hands on her." When the father continued trying to save her, the policeman killed him.

How can you ignore or forget stuff like that?

I also saw an act of kindness. It also involved a kid. It was raining and cold. He looked to be a teenager of maybe fourteen or fifteen and he wasn't dressed warm. He was standing under the eaves of this store. The owner of the store came out and saw the boy standing there. He said, "What you gonna do? Break into my store?" The boy said, "No, I'm cold." A cop came running, billy stick in hand, to see if the store owner needed help. At that time, I believed that under those uniforms were the same old Klansmen. They just traded the Klan for the police department. It was just my theory at the time because there was just so much brutality going on. The boy walked away and disappeared around the corner while the store owner kept talking loudly to the cop about sports and some sort of new dance, all the while glancing over his shoulder from time to time. I realized later that the owner kept talking to the cop in order to protect the child by giving him a chance to leave. The boy was very lucky.

One time a fellow was coming down the street right outside of my father's store. It was in the summer and he didn't have on nothing but his pants. A cop came along and jammed his stick in the man's bare stomach. The man threw up and then the cop took the stick and started beating him up with it. I couldn't look anymore.

There were some white folks that didn't like what they'd seen, and once it was over, they'd come up to a black person and say so.

I've never forgotten how all of that felt. Stuff like that sticks with you.

On August 28, 1963, I went to the March on Washington where I heard Dr. Martin Luther King's "I Have a Dream" speech. At first, I was afraid to go because I thought there might be rioting. Whether the rioters would be black or white was really not the point. I am a tiny person and would be easily trampled by an angry crowd of any color. So I thought about how much Laura and Cheryl still needed me and decided that Dr. King would understand if I stayed home in New York City. I was working as a clerk in the records room at Harlem Hospital at the time. One of my coworkers rented a bus and sold tickets to whoever wanted to go. Two of my friends bought tickets and planned to travel together. At the last minute, one of them had to bow out because something was wrong with her husband and she had to stay at home. So I said a prayer to the Lord to help me get back to my daughters, took the woman's place, and got on the bus. The event was very nice, but I realized that we were surrounded by the police and hoped that no one did anything which would cause them to charge the crowd.

When Dr. King came out, we gave him our full attention. I admired Dr. King before that day as a great man who was fighting for our freedom as well as trying to enlighten Americans and wake them up. He was very much trying to uplift people in the same way that Malcolm X tried to do.

Dr. King passionately explained his vision of what could happen if there was justice in the country for *all* Americans. What I don't understand is why the same parts of the speech have been quoted over and over again throughout these many years. He said so much more. I liked the part when he talked about what America owed the black people. He talked about it like he was holding a promissory note that it was time for the country to honor. "In a sense, we've come to our nation's capital to cash a check. When the architects of our republic wrote the magnificent words of the Constitution and the Declaration of Independence, they were signing a promissory note to which every American was to fall heir . . . It is obvious that America has defaulted on this promissory note, insofar as her citizens of color are concerned. Instead of honoring this sacred obligation, America has given the Negro people a bad check, a check which has come back marked 'insufficient funds.'"

By the time he finished speaking, I was in awe of him, totally blown away, moved to tears, and with a feeling in my chest that had no name. I believed in him. I feared for him. I wanted him to succeed. I absolutely and totally loved him.

When evening set in, everyone headed toward the buses. My friend and I had been given the wrong information about the parking location and we went the wrong way. We couldn't find the bus and it left Washington, DC, without us. Luckily the two of us had extra money because we had to find the regular bus station and buy tickets for a bus that was not going to leave for two hours. We sat in the station feeling tired and anxious, but finally it was time to board and I got home.

Malcolm X was upright and outspoken. He spoke on corners on 125th Street and on 116th Street too. Sometimes I would take the girls with me. Cheryl says, "We went to hear him speak a lot. While I didn't understand everything he was saying, it felt like church because of the call and response. He was a great speaker. I remember when Mom took us to view his body at Unity Funeral Home in Harlem. When I looked in the casket, he looked quite red. His hair and skin were lighter than I had seen from a distance when we were watching him from the crowds. I knew that he was a big figure in the civil rights movement. You know I did like going to hear Malcolm because his passion triggered something in me. I could not figure it all out but the places were always packed shoulder to shoulder with people. Everyone was on their feet and it was all very emotionally charged. I liked the fire that he had in him before his trip to Mecca, but I liked the calm Malcolm who came back after his realization that there was more kindness in the world than hatred. I underwent a similar change. I studied abroad during my junior year, and when I came back, I was different and I knew that I saw the world differently. It was a much more balanced view of how we are all connected as human beings. I think that is what happened to Malcolm."

I didn't take the girls with me to political speeches all the time because I didn't want to influence their beliefs too much. I went by myself for twenty minutes or so when I got a chance. All of the speakers had their street corner pulpits on different street corners right there in Harlem. I usually only had to walk a few blocks. One year, I heard Malcom X speak at least twice a week at different places in Harlem, including the Audubon Ballroom where he was eventually gunned down (twenty-one bullets in his chest alone) on February 21, 1965, at the age of thirty-nine. The public viewing of his body was held at Unity Funeral Home in Harlem. The line to get in was around several corners. It was all very somber and sad.

People think it is odd when I talk about how lucky I was to get me and my children an apartment in the St. Nicholas Houses, a Harlem housing project. What has been forgotten is just how hard it was for black people to find any kind of housing at all, let alone affordable housing with other rooms to keep everyone from being on top of one another. The turmoil caused by our attempts to find decent housing was repeated time and again after World War II. When the black soldiers came home from fighting, they thought that having helped to defeat the Nazis would give them some kind of prestige in society. Marriage and starting families were foremost in the minds of many veterans, and with this came the need to secure housing. They had a rude awakening coming to them.

In years past, our folks had been forced to live on land that no one else wanted, usually on the outskirts of cities. After the war, things shifted. I don't understand all that happened to cause the shift, but somebody invented the suburbs.

Now listen at this.

They wanted us off that land outside the city so that white folk could live in the cities. Through rezoning laws, practices of redlining, collusion between mortgage lending agencies, insurance companies, and real estate entities, our folks found themselves either being priced out of their homes or prevented from making such purchases.

Then, since the war was over, the arms industry started laying people off. Everyone (whites included) started getting laid off and forced into the ranks of unemployment. Since whites were deserting the cities and going to the suburbs, blacks were forced to find housing in parts of Northern cities that were being abandoned.

Clearly Northern racism was a force to be reckoned with when it came to the same type of Southern Jim Crow segregation.

What became to be known as "white flight" reduced urban locations to zones of economic despair.

With the rise of President Lyndon B. Johnson in the aftermath of John F. Kennedy's November 22, 1963 assassination, a new era came into view. With President Johnson's programs, federal power was expanded to create job opportunities, provide access to education, bolster the actual enforcement of civil rights, and ensure housing for all poor people, not just black people as most people believe.

My daughters both benefited greatly from two parts of President Johnson's grand vision. He wanted to level the playing field so that smart young people did not have to miss out on college if they simply happened to be poor. Enter the Educational Opportunities Programs (EOP) which helped Laura and Cheryl get their undergraduate degrees. EOP had several plans, but the ones that my girls took advantage of required that they get accepted to a college based solely on grades and merit. Once that was accomplished and they could prove that they came from a very low-income household, they had had access to low-interest loans. I was making only four thousand dollars a year at the time so they were actually eligible for free tuition. They also got work study grants as part of their financial aid package. These kids were not just granted freebies. President Johnson wanted to see that they had some skin in the game and that skin came in the form of working on campus and taking at least one loan for books and supplies, which, though low interest, still had to be paid back.

When Cheryl went to law school, she was able to attend only because another program called Model Cities gave her a grant of three thousand dollars. Sadly, that program (like so many others) is no longer around. But they really worked. When Cheryl finished college and law school, she was only in debt for $5,500. Laura owed even less. The only thing that saddened me about the whole higher education thing was that Cheryl was originally accepted to the Ivy League school, Smith College. They interviewed her four or five times and paid her travel fees to the school each time. She wanted very badly to attend that school, and when they wanted her, we were all very excited. Then the financial aid package came and our hopes were dashed. Even with scholarships and grants, which were generous, because that was an expensive school, I still would have had to pay eight hundred dollars every single year of her four years there. The amount that they said I had to come up with might seem small, but they may as well have been asking me for eight thousand dollars per month for four years. Either one was impossible. There was just no way to get that money every year.

In the end, Cheryl went to college in Ithaca, New York, and got a BA in political science. She was very happy there. My athletic girl had found a college that had a ski slope and even a fancy fountain in the library. The school was known for communications and music, so the music school looked like the philharmonic. It was really beautiful. She originally wanted to be a biochemist and then, after studying abroad in England for a year, she came back and changed her major and career direction.

I don't know why the government did not continue with the Model Cities Program. It shut down after only three or four years. Cheryl got money from them the whole time she was in law school.

A lot of those programs were set up to equalize the disparity between blacks and whites. Johnson's Great Society was just that. It was the best.

One of his other programs helped Cheryl get her first real job. She had just graduated from college when a new Johnson plan went into effect. In June of 1973, a program was started at Ithaca College that worked with high school students who were failing. Cheryl got a full-time job as the head female counselor and had twenty-two counselors reporting to her. She also taught Spanish and Tae Kwon Do.

But poor President Johnson and the power of his office was simply no match for the poisoned hearts of those who were adamant that blacks would not fully participate in the nation's economy. Such entities proved immeasurably creative in making sure that urban blacks were confined to warehouse-like living spaces in which opportunity, economy, education, and hope had fled to the suburbs.

With no economic investment and reinvestment in the black communities, hardworking folks were trying to stir the ocean with a spoon.

There was surely hope that it could be done, but there were few who could afford to wait for that eventuality. In the meantime, decay happened just as it always does when human beings of any color find themselves with few options and devoid of hope.

Tired and sad, President Johnson announced in 1968 that he would not seek re-election, and in that year, the victory went to Richard M. Nixon.

We all know what happened next. 'Nuff said.

I hope that someday racism won't exist at all.

We all have one thing in common whether we are black, white, or any other color. Everyone wants a great life for their children.

THE STICKUP MAN

With my meager paycheck

tucked tightly in my jeans.

Walking quietly with my thoughts

of tomorrow and things to be done

bills to pay, plans to make with

daylight gone and evening upon me

I didn't realize the distance I had traveled

until I heard

this is a stick up.

A stick up.

I heard myself saying it

not realizing I was in danger

at that moment.

I had to think fast.

What street is this?

I ask as in a daze.

Two men snatch at

my pocketbook.

What did they look like?

It happened so fast.

One had a hood top.

In the meantime
we both heard a police siren
getting closer.
So he ran in the other direction.
I ran to the nearest bus stop
just to find I was going the wrong way.

CHAPTER 10

THE WAY THINGS
MIGHT HAVE BEEN

One of my favorite Bible tales has always been the story of Job. I never understood why that story always moved me so much. Can it be that the Universe pulled me to it because someday I was going to need it?

Scripture states that in one day, Job, one of the wealthiest men of his region (Uz) and father of seven sons and three daughters, heard the following news:

One day when his sons and daughters were eating and drinking wine in the eldest brother's house, a messenger came to Job and said, "The oxen were plowing and the donkeys were feeding beside them, and the Sabeans fell on them and carried them off, and killed the servants with the edge of the sword; I alone have escaped to tell you." While he was still speaking, another came and said, "The fire of God fell from heaven and burned up the sheep and the servants, and consumed them; I alone have escaped to tell you." While he was still speaking, another came and said, "The Chaldeans formed three columns, made a raid on the camels and carried them off, and killed the servants with the edge of the sword; I alone have escaped to tell you." While he was still speaking, another came and said, "Your sons and daughters were eating and drinking wine in their eldest brother's house, and suddenly a great wind came across the desert, struck the four corners of the house, and it fell on the young people, and they are dead; I alone have escaped to tell you."

—Job 1:13–19 NRSV

In the space of one day, Job had lost his children and all that made him a wealthy man. One can only imagine the psychological and emotional trauma of losing one's family and lifetime of work and labor in the space of twenty-four hours. It didn't help that Job was an older man, and even he knew the dim likelihood of his being able to restore all that he had achieved/acquired over the course of his lifetime.

So began the journey of Job, who tried to make sense of his predicament, because it makes no sense that such calamity could have befallen him when it's noted that Job "was blameless and upright, one who feared God and turned away from evil" (Job 1:1 NRSV).

Job was understandably overwhelmed with despair, confusion, anger, and rage with the God whom he'd served so faithfully. But he never cursed God nor lost his ultimate belief in God's goodness.

In the end, Job's faith made all things knowable and proved

to be the source of his ability to endure calamity. Such was and is the case with me. My faith in the ultimate justice, grace, and mercy of the God of the universe was about to give me a rung to cling to in my most desperate moment of trial, and my deep faith was about to propel me through tragedy into a deeper relationship with my God.

If my sons wouldn't have been murdered, I would have followed the retirement plan that I had been dreaming of for years. First, I was going to travel and get to know the grandchildren of my siblings in a way that I could not do with a hectic work schedule. Just as my daughters were no longer really close, the same thing had happened between me and my own brothers and sisters. They all had their own husbands, wives, children, and grandchildren. It made sense that they were busy with their immediate families and we were not so close with each other anymore. My sisters and brothers had developed new ways of being and doing things once they became part of other families.

For example, my older sister had allowed her daughter to grow up with few rules or restraints. She wasn't a bad kid at all. I just wondered why Omena didn't stick with the program that Mama and Daddy had started.

That program was rigid but it worked. Go to church. Obey your parents. Work as many jobs as you can as early as you can. Don't talk back. Obey the law and the rules of whatever institution that you find yourself in. Never lie, and slacking was not to be tolerated. When I say it worked, I mean that we all turned out to be decent, law abiding citizens who didn't violate the rights of our fellow man, didn't go to jail, never accepted charity if we could help it, and raised kids just like us. Why change a winning strategy?

One time, many years ago, Omena and her husband were having a problem. Two of my younger sisters had the audacity to pack her and up bring her to my door where I was living in the St. Nicholas housing project. I didn't have a spare room, but since Omena had a daughter and I had two daughters, there were no sensitive gender issues to consider. So the girls shared one of the beds, my sister slept on the sofa in the living room, and I still had my own room.

Let's just say that when they came to live with me, they brought bad habits with them.

For example, my girls were accustomed to going to bed at nine o'clock. Omena's daughter stayed up until all hours. Her daughter sometimes came home from school, and instead of immediately doing her homework, she knocked on the door and asked, "Is my mother here?" before she decided whether to come in or go outside and play. It was a game the child was playing. She knew very well that her mother was at work and that her mother knew our household schedule and habits. Sometimes, it would be the middle of the night before that girl started laying out her clothes and getting ready for the next day. I could not let Laura and Cheryl start trying to behave that way.

Omena and her daughter had to go.

The problem was that Omena wanted me to let the housing authority know that she and her daughter were staying with me so that she could get on the waiting list for an apartment in the St. Nicholas Houses.

I told her, "Your name can stay here until you get your problem solved, but you have to find another place to actually stay."

So, she went and found a room for herself and her child until she got a call from the projects that a one-bedroom apartment had been found for them.

That is how my sister and I both ended up living in the St. Nicholas Houses. Because she lived nearby, we often talked about how spread out the family had become. We had siblings in Atlanta, Virginia, St. Croix, and lots of other places. I sadly thought how easy it would be for all our adult children to lose touch with each other and with their second and third cousins. When I retired, I was going to visit every single home and stay for a few weeks until I understood and celebrated who we had become. In other words, who their children and grandchildren were aside from the pictures that I received on holidays.

I also wanted to spend some time with my sisters and brothers reminiscing about our early years. Yes, we were poor, but we had such good times together when we were children. I wanted to talk about Mama and Daddy. Did they have memories that I didn't have? Of course. Each one of us had our own relationship with Mama and Daddy. Each one of us had our own interpretations of everything that had happened and not happened when we were growing up. I wanted to hear those stories.

Another dream of mine was to learn everything I could about black history both here in America as well as in the Caribbean. Ever since the days of hearing Marcus Garvey preach on the streets of Harlem, I had been interested in black empowerment. Now I had the time to visit the library and bookstores to quench my thirst for information about black people. Being without our identity is no excuse for being without our history. Plenty of very good writers of all nationalities had explored our past and I wanted to read their books. I also planned to become a regular at the Schomburg library, which was located at 135th Street and Lenox Avenue in Manhattan and devoted to black culture. I also remembered the many times I had passed the Black Liberation Bookstore on 131st Street and Lenox Avenue, wishing that I had time to read books by the armful. It is not enough to think of black history one month of every year. All Americans should think about it as a matter of course.

One time, when I was on my way home from some factory job, I passed a street-corner orator on 125th Street, which is the main shopping area in Harlem. He was shouting about our history. I stopped for a moment to rest and got caught up in the story. He was talking about how our story was such a rich one and included many inventors, scientists, mathematicians, astronomers, and leaders. I had no idea who the people were that he was referring to and started to walk away, but then I got caught up in a story he started telling about a man named Toussaint L'Ouverture. As a slave child, he was worried about not being strong. His dad acknowledged that he had been born small but advised him to get strong on his own without anyone else's help and that this would gain him freedom. It was the part about independence (which my father had preached incessantly) that held my attention. In other words, his father did not advise him to consult with anyone else to find the answer to his problem. He knew that the answer (if there was one to be had, given their constraints) laid within his son. Well, anyway, Mr. Toussaint apparently didn't forget the advice. He ended up defeating the French and set up the nation of Haiti.

I didn't have hours to spend reading these stories, and I certainly didn't have the money to buy books when the girls were young. So occasionally, I would stop and listen to a few minutes' oration from the young, nameless men who somehow learned these stories and just preached them on the streets of Harlem.

Benjamin Banneker's story was not as dramatic. I just couldn't understand how a poor boy, a son of a free black and an ex-slave, could become a mathematician and astronomer. It made me feel lazy and unaccomplished by comparison. While my background was lacking in many ways, I certainly could not claim to have been as low on society's rung as Mr. Toussaint or Mr. Banneker, yet they had accomplished amazing things and I had not. What was it that made these people so much more ambitious than I ever was or aspired to be?

These were the kinds of stories that I only heard in stolen moments of time as I went about my business of working hard and child rearing. I wanted to learn as much as I could in this area after I retired and had all the time in the world on my hands.

I planned to start with Harriet Tubman. Out of all the stories that I had heard, hers stuck in my head for a very long time. She was born in slavery but managed to run away and stay free. Then she decided to come back more than once to rescue others and show them a way out of slavery. I wanted to know where she got that kind of courage, bravery, and determination. I admired her more than I could say. Once I retired, I was going to treat myself to reading every word about her that had ever been published.

Visit family and learn history. Those were just two of the things I wanted to do once I had plenty of leisure time.

The year was 1977, and I was sixty-two and three years away from retirement. I was working at Harlem Hospital, a clerk in a department where over two hundred people were responsible for the care and maintenance of patients' records. The work was simply routine, not challenging at all. After all I'd been through, it was sort of fine by me that I didn't have to work my brain too hard to do a good job. What got on my nerves was the cattiness, pettiness, silly little jealousies, gossiping, and backbiting amongst my co-workers.

I wasn't really able to do anything to improve my situation. I was too afraid to take early retirement and quit. What I was most probably going to do was complain about the ridiculous mini-dramas that occurred in that department each day and long for three years to go by so that I could really feel safe enough to let go of a steady paycheck.

Well, most of the time it is something small that tips the scale. Something that doesn't seem like much to an outsider but is just what you need to do.

That day came for me when my daughter Cheryl, who at this point called herself Shelley, stopped by the record room. She was well groomed, clearly educated, and maybe had a fancy way of speaking, I don't know. She came to take me out for a surprise lunch.

I expressed my delight regarding her thoughtful invitation. Cheryl smiled and said, "Come on, Mom. I'm double parked."

In other words, my Cheryl had a car!

Some of my troublemaking co-workers wanted to know where Cheryl worked. I told them that she was a law-school student who was home for Easter vacation.

This was too much for that jealous crew. Most of their adult children had not gone to college, let alone law school.

They didn't know that Cheryl's car was a ragged Oldsmobile that she was hoping would last till graduation.

Five words: "I'm double parked" and "law school" caused jealousy to kick in.

Suspicious, someone asked, "Don't you have two daughters?"

"Yes," I answered proudly. "Laura is at Washington University getting her PhD..

This was way too much for them.

A woman named Nora promptly told me that I shouldn't be working in the record room. I told her that I was fine and that maybe she shouldn't be there either.

The whole thing was ridiculous.

After that day, I could hear whispering when I passed. Once again, it was assumed that I thought I was better than everyone else just because I had taught my kids to look beyond their surroundings and at the blue, limitless sky above.

I started waking up feeling sad. Then I began to see the scenes for the ridiculous theater that they were and started making believe that I was off to the circus.

So after Christmas of 1977, I finally filed the papers. It was official. I was going to retire.

What did I need the headache for?

I was proud of my girls. Laura would go on to head two separate chapters of the National Urban League. Cheryl would become a successful businesswoman specializing in high-end real-estate transactions in addition to her job at Fieldston and races of her own.

I was very proud of my girls, but it was time to focus on myself. I made my list of things that I would do in my retirement, and I assure you that becoming a professional runner was not on it.

I had been working in the records room at Harlem Hospital for many years by the time I was sixty-two. During my time there, I remember hearing lots of stories about patients who never received any visitors in homes for the elderly. Imagine being unable to care for yourself but still mentally fit. In other words, perhaps hanging off the edge of a wheelchair and remembering your children, friends, and old neighbors. Imagine wondering if everyone in the world has forgotten that you exist. Stories like that used to make me tear up something awful. I vowed to visit people who could not leave the facilities and didn't have any anyone to come see them. I would talk to them, and, hopefully make them laugh just a little bit.

I also wanted to be a volunteer in some way for the Democratic Party. I didn't know how to go about doing that, but I figured they must need people to answer phones and stuff envelopes or something. I'd been a Democrat since 1933 when I decided that Franklin Roosevelt was a good man and it was time to give back or maybe find a way to get more Americans to vote Democrat.

But most of all, I wanted to have time to go to the gym, then come home and write poem after poem after poem. I had fallen in love with poetry in elementary school and let the interest go by the wayside during the years after we left the shelter, when just keeping a roof over my young boys' heads was a big accomplishment. I never really went back to it until I retired, and then I bought a few books of poetry. I even wrote a few poems myself.

At the time, I didn't know why I liked poems so much. I've

thought about it a great deal since those days and I think it was because the poems that moved me emotionally were always about something hard, something sad, or some great wish. It feels good to know that others have tussled with sadness and won, or that others have great dreams that they can talk about in ways that feel like trees waving. I think that I loved it because in a story, the writer tells you straight out what he means. The poet doesn't do that. The poem means something different to everyone who reads it. I found that the hard part of writing a poem was figuring out a way to suggest something. I never learned to talk around a subject or to hint at something. With poetry, I had to learn how to hint.

The House

It was a lean-to shack
not far from the railroad track
overcrowded for its size
underkept
badly in need of repair.
The roof leaks.
Ceiling sags.
The floor squeaks and walls
crack.
Windows rattle.
Knobless doors open after a battle.
The house that once held plenty
of love and controlled finance.
A lot of laughter.
Is now a house of chance.

I must take into consideration
the lengthy cast of moderation.
Be it ever so humble.
There's no place like home.
Today's world
filled with druggies and junkies of all ages,
    sizes, colors
abusing anyone they can to fulfill their
    corrupt diet. I get
the feeling someday soon
everything will calm down to
an unbelievable quiet.

Before I could sink into my hard-won retirement and fully indulge my love for both history and poetry, family duty called again. But this was something I was overjoyed to do for one of my nieces. My brother Nolas had a married daughter named Lydia who had been going to college trying to earn a bachelor's in sociology when her husband, a career military man, accepted a transfer from Missouri to San Antonio, Texas. The couple was raising their thirteen-year-old daughter and Lydia's younger sister who was a freshman in high school. The four of them moved to San Antonio and Lydia enrolled in a college there. The only problem was they would not let her transfer all of her college credits from Missouri. Lydia needed to go back and finish her last semester, but her husband traveled a great deal and there was no one in San Antonio to stay with her girls.

When I heard about Lydia's predicament, I thought, *Here we go again*. I remembered back to the time I was so close to earning my high school diploma, only to have it snatched away from me. I remembered Cheryl getting accepted to a top tier school like Smith College but being unable to go because I couldn't afford the eight hundred dollars. I did not want to see this happen again. To make matters worse, Lydia had married young and I had heard that it wasn't a good union. It would be a monumental thing if I could help her out, because clearly getting an education was very important to her. I had learned the hard way that women should have their own professional careers that paid well enough for them to have freedom. I didn't want Lydia to be trapped and financially dependent on this man or any other man. I needed her to know that her Aunt Ida understood her striving to accomplish something.

Without hesitation, I contacted her with an offer. I would go take care of her husband and children in San Antonio for six months while she did what she needed to do. Once she earned her degree, I would come back to New York and she could take over the care of her family.

Happily, my niece agreed and off (the year must have been 1978) I went.

San Antonio is located about seventy-five miles southwest of Austin, the state capital. At that time, the population was something like 650,000 and black people made up a miniscule part of the population. When I arrived, it was a mild winter although it got very cool at night. I can only remember a few times when the temperature dipped very low, although it never reached the freezing temperature that I was accustomed to in New York City. San Antonio had a lot of military bases and I think someone told me that there were more bases there than anywhere else in the United States.

Lydia's husband had been in active Air Force duty in Missouri and was going to be doing the same thing in San Antonio. They got me a temporary military ID card so that I could use the commissary. Since I am a pretty sociable person, I got to know the neighbors and often visited with them. Since I didn't know how to drive, they took me wherever I needed to go when Lydia's husband was out of town. Lydia's friend Carol was simply wonderful. She took me and the girls to the movies and did lots of other fun stuff for us. I didn't have to worry about their transportation to and from school because there was a school bus which serviced the subdivision where Lydia lived. They didn't live on Randolph Air Force Base where the husband was stationed. Instead, they owned a pretty and spacious house in a section called Universal City.

Once Lydia received her degree, her husband got an overseas assignment. She decided to use her degree to get into the military and they gave her an age waiver. There were not a lot of minority women, but she went overseas with him as an officer and not a dependent wife. I clapped my hands and shouted when I got the news. At first, she intended to stay in the service for only four years, but she ended up doing the entire twenty years and retired as a lieutenant colonel. She also got out of the bad marriage. Lydia met her second husband while on active duty in Germany and they have now been married for twenty-nine years.

CHAPTER 11

MOTHERS AND SONS

A Pain So Deep

From before the dawn of time, it was decided in the councils of heaven that the bond between mothers and sons would be one that could withstand any test, overcome any trial, endure any hardship, suffer all setbacks, navigate any complexities, hurdle all obstacles, triumph over any number and variety of foes, purify the most perfect love, ingest and digest all insults, forgive all wrongs, embrace in all seasons, times, and circumstances, and grow ever stronger, broader, and deeper.

For even in those cases where mothers and sons are bound together in such relationships that may appear toxic to observers, the roiling waters of those connections are still governed by the glue that has united mothers to the hearts of their sons and sons to the hearts of their mothers since the beginning of time.

Attempts to quantify or qualify the origins of the love that a mother has for her son are worthy but, ultimately, fruitless exercises. All that can be said with any degree of accuracy is that a mother's love for her son is consigned to the realm of mystery, wonder, and admiration. For along stories of mothers who perform what strikes observers as superhuman feats of strength to protect her children, that strength is multiplied exponentially when that child is a son. Likewise, when a father is protecting his daughter, the reality of his protective instincts moves the blood in him to surge with greater power to fulfill the role assigned to him long ago when humans were sitting around fires in caves, learning the fundamentals of their species.

How else can one explain the stories of parents charging into harm's way to save their children?

In the year 1856, Margaret Garner, an African American slave woman in Kentucky, attempted to escape with her family across the Ohio River into the Northern state of Ohio. Slave hunters were hot on the family's trail, so Margaret and her loved ones took refuge in the home of an ally of the Underground Railroad. As the serial-raping, man-stealing, cradle-plundering, women-whipping, soul-stripping tyrants closed in on the family, Margaret Garner cut the throat of her two-year-old daughter. She wounded the other three of her children, but they survived.

The love that compelled Margaret Garner to spare her children's life in misery in exchange for bliss in death was, and is, but a sample of the depths to which a mother will go to save her son. Go to any courtroom in America, and there'll be mothers pleading with officers of the court to spare their sons even spending one day being caught in the merciless grip of the US system of jurisprudence.

Visit any military cemetery across the great expanse of the

American homeland and there's a great possibility of seeing a mother crying fresh, bitter tears for the son she bore who gave his last full measure for a nation that may not even remember his name.

Eavesdrop on any household where an enraged, inebriated father turns his abusive intention to a mother's son, and listen to the whirlwind of courage and conflict that ensues when the son's mother comes to his aid and rescue. Likewise, if that father moves to heap abuse onto the mother, if the son is old enough, strong enough, and feeling the quickening of his own dawning man-hood, he won't hesitate to position himself between the abuser and his mother, and willingly commit to a battle royal to spare from harm the one who literally gave him birth.

Move quietly through any hospital ward where a mother sits anxiously at the bedside of her male child. With agony bottled up for fear of shouting the roof down, and with eyes red from tears cried from depths unknown, and a tongue tired from imploring heaven to intervene, that mother will be united in a spiritual plane inhabited by her and son and intolerant of anyone else.

When the mother-son connection is healthy and thriving, it serves as a great incubator of hope and happiness being prepared for that woman who will someday, one day, share the son's life as his girlfriend, and possibly, wife. For any woman seeking to know what her life might be like with the man of her dreams, she should look first at the relationship that her dreamboat has with his mother. If he treats Mom well, loves her, respects her, and seeks to ensure that she's cared for, protected, and otherwise free (as much as possible) of worries, then a future wife has been gifted with a preview of how such a son will be when he becomes her husband.

There are no examples in all the recollections of the world that perfectly demonstrate the pureness of love between mother and son as that which existed between Jesus, the Christ, and his mother, Mary.

From the moment she was overshadowed by the Holy Spirit and conceived, Mary's motherhood was to be unique from all mothers who'd come before her and all those who'd follow. The stellar nature of her character, her purity of heart, and deep, powerful well of faith had not slipped the attention of God who chose her to be the vessel who would bear his Son, the Savior of the world.

The circumstances of Jesus' birth, entering the world in a ramshackle barn while being sought by some of the wisest and wealthiest kings of the day, bespoke the peculiar nature of the life Jesus would live. By all accounts, this son of a carpenter was like other children. He played. He could be mischievous. He could be a handful. And he was precocious.

The elders of Israel discovered soon enough that Jesus was not just another child. He understood the laws of Israel and obeyed the customs and traditions of his people as someone who'd been their author as much as he was their practitioner. Mary could not help being proud as her young son grew into manhood, and as the prophecy foretold, first assumed his place among his people and then launched a movement that challenged his brethren to love the Lord their God in a new way.

Mercy was the new rule of the day. Grace, the unmerited favor of God, was the longed-for ground of assurance that God had staked out in the living embodiment of his son. Love was the first, last, and only worthwhile measure that could completely capture the attention of the Savior. His words inspired the down-trodden to have hope, the wicked to reform, the hopeless to lift their eyes, the outcasts to know they were preferred among his friends, and the beleaguered of this world to find refuge in him.

From her vantage point as mother of a grown man who was the living Son of God, Mary understood that there would come a day and hour when her faith would be tested. For she understood that the world in which she lived could not, and would not, tolerate a message from anyone, especially a lowly Nazarene carpenter's boy, that the laws of Israel had passed their usefulness, and the new laws were literally wrapped up in him.

Such was the love of Mary for her Son that she could pray and hope for him as he entered into his greatest time of trial. Such was the devotion of Mary to the Christ whom she'd borne that she shadowed his journey on the way to Calvary's bloodstained hill.

Standing there that day, casting her distraught gaze onto the beaten and battered body of her Son, Mary's heart must have broken a million, million times, as she recalled the good times when she'd sung him to sleep. The dams holding her tears proved inadequate to the task as she recalled his little boy hugs of adoration. The strength in her legs must've fled upon the realization that murderous elements had conspired to take away her precious son, and there was nothing she could do about it.

She'd be left alone without her Jesus. She'd be a woman without her beloved special son, but the bond showed itself forever durable, for Jesus had one more act to perform to assure the healing of his mother's heart. Looking down from the cross with his life fast ebbing, he looked at Mary, then the disciple named John, and said, "Woman, here is your son," and to John, "Here is your mother."

Scripture states with declarative certainty that "from that time on, this disciple [John] took her into his own home." Mary had cared for him for so long in so many ways. Now that he was leaving her, he suspended the flight of his life to ensure having enough time and energy to guarantee that his beloved mother would not be left alone and destitute.

Then, the Lord Jesus died.

The next phase of the fabulous story of history's most famous mother and son connection involved the resurrection of Jesus who, with his return to be forever among the living, declared himself King of Kings and Lord of Lords. The salvation that Jesus' death offered to all of humanity had a special stamp of invitation upon it for Mary, the mother whose love, lessons, and life had been the source of his existence up till the day he'd been moved by the Holy Spirit to fulfill his role as the Son of God.

The mystery of the love that bound Jesus to Mary while she'd carried him in her womb was just as strong as the day she watched him being assassinated upon the cross. That mysterious love simultaneously pulled forth tears of heartbreak while fortifying her with the knowledge that the great crime perpetrated against the Christ was something that had been foretold and now required being endured. And lastly, the mystery of the love between Mary and the Christ which saw her draw strength from him as he drew strength from her in the closing moments of his life, has throughout history served as the finest example of the mysterious love binding mothers to sons and sons to mothers, in the great trials, triumphs, and winding journeys of the great adventure called *life*.

I don't know when or how my sons, Donald and Charles, got involved in the world of illegal drugs, but I do know that I warned them to stay away from street life early and often.

Donald, the eldest boy that Rip and I brought into this world, was born on May 15, 1937. Donald had a confusing childhood because Rip's mother was obsessed with him and determined to turn him against me so that she could convince him to move in with her and Danny, her husband. I'm sure the problem started when she declared him her prince the first time she laid eyes on him as a newborn with his full head of curly, black hair. He went from a cute baby to a truly good-looking boy, who at first looked just like his father.

Since he was my first child, our bond during his childhood could have been stronger. I loved him and I'm sure that he loved me too, but Rip's mother and father were his babysitters and they talked bad about me to Donald every chance they got. Worse, his paternal grandmother constantly told him that I didn't love him at all and didn't want him around. Since regular, reliable childcare was always a challenge and they didn't charge me any money, I left him with them far more than I would have liked.

Two years after his birth, my second son, Charles, was born which probably created more distance between me and Donald. As a result of all this, he and I sometimes had a difficult relationship. When he was a tiny boy, I could sometimes feel his dislike. I could also tell that he was being told hurtful things to say to me. He was only three years old when he looked me square in the face and said, "I can't wait until you're dead so that I can go live with my grandmother." What small child can put together an idea and a sentence like that? Rip's mother had to have told him to say that. When he was nine years old, he said something along those same lines. Since he wasn't a baby anymore, I gave him his wish. I packed a suitcase and took him bag and baggage to Rip's mother. I hoped that he would see that being a visitor in someone's home and actually living there were two entirely different things. Unfortunately, it didn't work out that way. I went and got him after a few weeks, but thereafter, he was always back and forth between us. It was like Rip's mother and I had joint custody or something.

When Donald became a teenager, he once again made it clear that he preferred to stay with her and not with me. This time he did not come back home.

Donald did not move into the St. Nicholas Houses with me. My poor oldest son had been so messed up. All of his life, his grandmother was telling him one thing, his father was telling him another thing, and I chimed in with a third. Rip's mother was a horrible woman to disrupt Donald's life like that. They loved it that Donald looked like Rip when he was a little boy, while Charles looked like me. Once, I said to Rip's mother, "Eventually both of the boys are going to look like me. Then what you gonna do?"

His attitude cut me to the quick and I wondered if Rip's mother really understood that turning a child against his mother does not do anything good for that child's spirit. She hurt me but she hurt the person she supposedly loved so much a whole lot more.

A bunch of people cannot raise one child unless they're all using the same methods. I kept saying, "I'm his mother. His best interests come from me and not from you telling him, 'You don't have to do this,' and, 'Your mother don't like you'—all these kind of lies."

The Richardsons deliberately interfered with the relationship between me and my son with disastrous results.

Sometimes she would imply spitefully that I was only so concerned about Donald because he looked like Rip and I still loved the man. Nothing could have been further from the truth. I told her that my boys have the same mother and the same father. I don't care who they look like. They didn't like my younger son because he looked like me, not his father. It didn't matter. In later years, both of my sons stayed more with their grandmother than they stayed with me. She won the battle and my sons paid the emotional price.

When Donald was in the third grade he went to school with sixty-five cents in his pocket and was targeted by people with drugs. Sixty-five cents is not a lot of money now, but you could buy quite a few things with that sum in 1945 when Donald was eight years old. Rip's parents were always giving him money even though I asked them to stop because a kid with money tends to attract the wrong people. His grandparents would do a lot of things for him, much more than they should have. They loved him and they spoiled him. I guess to them it was like having Little Boy Rip back again. Sometimes when I had to work two jobs, they would take care of Donald for days on end. They would only grudgingly keep Charles as well. I didn't see how this behavior was good for either of the boys, but there was nothing I could do about it because I needed to earn every penny that came my way.

When he was little, Rip's mother would say things to Donald like, "Yo mudda no good. She like Charles better."

CAN'T NOTHING BRING ME DOWN

I have to say that Donald never completely learned to hate me or totally turn his back on me. As a teenager, he always came around to spend time with me and the girls.

Donald went into the Navy in the mid-1950s. By then, he was a well-built man, tall at five-foot-ten with a deep chocolate complexion. I am told that the women loved him. Cheryl certainly did. Her eldest brother was her hero. Sometimes he would come home on leave without warning and Cheryl would be ecstatic. He did a three-year term in the Navy. When he got out, he was addicted to heroin.

My Donald was an artist. He could draw anything or anyone. Sometimes he drew pictures in charcoal, other times he created black and white sketches. He could not find an outlet for that talent or for his athletic ability. One of his demons was probably his inability to find a mode of expression. In any case, he married a woman named June when he was in his late twenties. They had one child which he named Darryl, which was Rip's real name. I could not understand why Donald would name the child after his father after all that Rip had put me through. It hurt my feelings but I kept my mouth shut. I didn't want to cause a rift in the delicate relationship that we had. In any case, the marriage between Donald and June lasted four years.

After the breakup, he started using heroin more heavily. I tried to talk to him about going to get some kind of help to rid his body of the craving for the dangerous drug. He would always promise to do it but I guess he never followed through. One day he called, and when my girls told him that I was not home, he came to the door with some guy. He told Laura and Cheryl that I had sold our television set to the guy and that they

166

had come to pick it up. Donald and his friend took the TV out of my apartment. Of course, he sold it to buy drugs. I finally got him on the phone and told him, "You cannot ever come back in the house." He was banned from the house for four years and then I started letting him come around again. Since he was still using drugs, I used to hide my purse whenever he came. On one occasion, he stole Laura's typewriter. I found it in the local pawn shop and bought it back. That was the last of Donald. He was totally banned.

I knew little to nothing of Donald's street life—what he did or who he lived with—until he got himself killed. Here is what happened as best my family and I can figure out.

He had a reputation in the street as a mean guy, a man that you did not cross if you had any sense at all. According to my eldest daughter, "Don't mess with Donald" was a warning to anyone who was just getting to know him. I don't know what he did to get such a fearsome reputation and I never want to know.

Anyhow, the story goes that he met this woman named Hilda who was a drug dealer in Queens over by Liberty Avenue. She had five children and together they had a sixth, a little girl. There was a number runner in Queens who wanted to get into the drug business. He sent his son to Hilda to say that if she didn't give her drug business to his father, his father would kill her and her children. This conversation took place in a bar where Donald was present. Since the number runner and his son had to know Donald's reputation and that he was Hilda's boyfriend, I can only assume that they wanted to goad Donald into doing something stupid so they could eliminate him. Anyway, Donald tapped the son on the shoulder and told him that he and his father were going to end up in motorized wheelchairs. Then he chased the guy out of the bar and shot him in the spine. The guy was in a motorized wheelchair after that and folks whispered that his father must have put a contract on Donald.

He called Cheryl and told her, "I'm just calling to let you guys know that I have something to do. These young punks want to test you. When you have a reputation, you only can ride so long on it. Twenty years is a long time. I have to do something and I may have to retire."

Cheryl asked, "Donald are you telling me that you are about to die?"

He said, "Just tell mother I love her."

"Tell Mother I love her." That part of this whole thing never fails to bring me to my knees in sorrow and gratitude. What it says to me is that despite everything that the Richardsons did to try and make my eldest child detest me, I was the one he thought about when he saw death coming. I was the only person that it appeared he left a message for. Oh! What I wouldn't give to let him know just what a heavy load that one sentence lifted from my heart. I wish that Donald had said that to me directly. It would have meant the world to me, and maybe with the air all cleaned up between us, we could have actually given each other a great big hug.

Was Donald afraid to tell me that he loved me? If so, what was he afraid of? Rejection from me would have meant that his grandparents were right all along. Maybe he was afraid of that.

I will never know.

The police arrested Hilda for something and she was not able to deal with being in jail. She was claustrophobic, had six kids, and wanted to get out in the worst way. While she was trying to find a way out of her troubles, Donald was found hanging in the basement of her house with no shoes on. It happened in July of 1978. His hands were tied behind his back and someone had given him a shot of heroin. A suicide note was found. In the note, he spelled his last name *Richardsen* which was the wrong spelling and could have been a signal that the note was written under duress.

An anonymous tip to the police led them to Donald's body.

Who made that call to the police and why? Whoever did it had to either have seen him die or heard about the murder from someone who saw him die. These were the thoughts that swirled around and around in my head. It almost drove me crazy. Donald had only one child with Hilda, and when he died, that little girl was not even two years old. Hilda kept in touch with me until the child was about five or six and then she moved away. I don't know what became of my granddaughter.

Two years passed and eight months passed and I was still not over the grief and pain caused by Donald's violent death and the fact that no one had ever been arrested for it. Then, the unthinkable happened.

Charles, my only remaining son, died violently as well.

Charles Richardson was born on May 6, 1939, the youngest boy born to me and Rip. He was a gentle boy who adored me so much that he called me Mother Dear instead of Mommy. He had a great sense of humor, and because of that, it was hard for me to get mad at him even when he was doing wrong. He was just so funny and loving that I always ended up laughing along with him. He was my baby boy and he never said cruel things to me like Donald did. I think that Charles was the gentler of the two because he had not been taught to dislike me as Donald had been.

He did okay in school until he became a teenager and the girls started chasing him. One girl named Betty was relentless. She was a pretty girl with clear skin, even features, pretty hair, and a shapely figure. He actually liked Betty a lot and she was always up in his face. She chased Charles so hard that he eventually became her boyfriend.

Like most teenage boys, Charles liked to dance, chase the girls, and have a good time. The only thing is that he started playing hooky to do these things and that just could not turn out well.

One day, Cheryl had stayed home from school because she was sick with the mumps. I was at work. Charles stopped by with ten or more teenagers. They put records on and danced. Cheryl watched as they started grinding, dancing very close together in a way that could easily become sexually suggestive. Nobody drank or smoked or used drugs. In fact, Charles and Betty were so wholesome, I used to call them "soda pop kids."

Anyway, when I got home, Cheryl told me all about it. "Mommy, Charles came today with a lot of friends.

I replied, "Oh, really? What did they do?"

"The girls were on the wall."

"Show me where."

There on the wall were stains from the grease on the girls' heads. Right above the grease marks were handprints. That meant that the boys had been leaning against the wall while pressing up close on the girls. That was one time where I was really angry and disappointed with Charles. He promised to never do that again, and, as far as I know he never did.

I was upset a while later when he decided that he'd had enough of school. I wouldn't sign him out, so he went to his father. Rip signed the papers and Charles was free from school at the age of sixteen. When I learned about this, I was very upset for two reasons. First of all, I did not know that Charles even had any relationship with Rip. It was the first time I had to actually sit back and think about it. Of course he and Donald both probably had a relationship with their father. After all, they had spent most of their time with their father's mother. Why was I so surprised? I guess it was because neither of them ever mentioned it.

The second reason I was upset was because Rip should have done everything he could to force Charles to stay in school. There were no decent jobs out there for kids without a high school diploma. No one knew that better than Rip and me. Instead of doing the hard work of helping Charles change his mind, Rip had taken the easy way out. Again. It made me sick.

Charles started seeing Betty again and she gave birth to three of his children, though they never married. He married a woman named Lucretia and they also had a son. Then he went into the service. When Charles was in the Army on the second tour, he was in Okinawa which was a shipping point for Vietnam. He refused to go and went AWOL. He spent a lot of time overseas, ducking the military police which strained his marriage to Lucretia. The military police caught up with him and he was sent to a place called Watertown. While he was at

Watertown, a dance troupe came through and he fell in love with a dancer called Mikki. Charles really loved her. When he was released from Watertown, they stayed together for seven or eight years.

These days I watch psychologists on TV talk about how important it is for boys to have their father in their lives to teach them how to be men. I don't know how living under the same roof with Rip, a lying adulterer with a gambling problem who never fought to keep in touch with them, could have saved my boys, but the thought has crossed my mind. I truly don't know what happened to Charles after that. I mean, how he got caught up in anything to do with drugs. Some have told me that he started hanging out with Donald and started going downhill from there. I just don't know.

Sometimes when I think about Charles, I remember how much he loved to cook and what a good dancer he was. He loved to dance. He would put a record on the record player and a smile would light up his eyes and mouth. Then he would either grab one of his delighted sisters and twirl her around or he would dance by himself with his eyes closed.

Anyway, Cheryl says that one night when Laura, Charles, and I were over at her place, he came into the kitchen to talk with her. He told her, "I was just looking around and wondering if something happened to me, who would be able to be here. I have a situation. I borrowed $1,100 from a guy because I was doing this deal with this cat. We could get this thing, step on it four times, and sell it to make $4,440. When we got it, the stuff was already stepped on . . . poor quality. So I still owe $1,100 and I have junk that I can't use."

Someone beat my Charles with a baseball bat. Naturally, when he got hurt, Cheryl thought that the culprit was the guy Charles owed $1,100. She went to speak with him. It turned out that he was a good friend of Charles's and Cheryl did not get the sense that he did it. The beating that Charles took was not about business. It was personal. There was something else going on in Charles's life that we will never know about.

When some of his childhood friends showed up at my house and Charles wasn't with them, I knew that something was wrong. They told me that he was hurt bad and in the hospital.

The beating took place on December 16, 1980. His brain was still in its case but it was just mush, no longer intact. By the time we got to the hospital, he was no longer talking. On December 20th, the plug to the machines that were keeping him barely alive was pulled. He died right away. The official cause of death was blunt force trauma to the head. Because of the holidays, he did not have a funeral until the 29th.

I think that it was for my sake that the family tried to act normal throughout the Christmas holidays, but I wasn't fooled. We were all hurting real bad.

No one knows if the $1,100 was connected to the killing. The beating took place on 144th Street and Seventh Avenue in broad daylight. All of the people on that street who were interviewed by the police claimed to have seen nothing. At the time of his death, Charles was working for the Department of Transportation giving out parking tickets. He wore the required brown uniform. It seemed to me that folks should remember who beat the traffic agent, but no one was talking.

Charles left four children behind.

After Charles's funeral, Cheryl sent me to visit my eldest daughter, Laura, who was in Missouri working toward her PhD. My blood pressure went through the roof so Cheryl told Laura to send me back to Harlem.

It didn't matter to me where I was. After I lost both my boys to drug related activity less than three years apart, I was just down in the dumps. My blood pressure wouldn't go down and nothing I tried seemed to make me feel any better. I could see the worry in Cheryl's face, but there was just nothing I could do. One day she stopped by and asked, "Why don't you just come and go with me on a mini race?" I thought nothin' else is workin', I'll just go on ahead.

It was my first race. I took off and all these people was rushin' past. It felt like somebody pulled a sheet off me; it was horrible, but I said I can't slow down now. I got to keep going. I started thinking this is too much, then all of a sudden, I started picking up a little speed and I thought, gee maybe this is good for me.

When I run, I feel relaxed and like I'm out with the wind.

Donald and Charles's deaths still hurt me even today. Donald loved to draw boats and people. He never really liked school but he was smart. In the end, all of my lectures about drugs and street life meant nothing. They went out there and started messing with the drugs anyway. When kids are small, you can control them. When they get older and once they go with their friends, you don't know what they are doing. They become secretive about everything, and you learn about it all only when something serious happens.

Donald and Charles did what they wanted to do and I couldn't stop them.

The loss of my sons was unbearable. I felt my whole world fall apart. One was almost forty and the other one was almost forty-two when they got killed. I could feel myself going lower and lower. I didn't even want to be here. I don't even like to think about it or talk about it. It's so hurtful.

SOAP STORY TO
ALL MY CHILDREN

As the world turns we enter

the days of our lives

realizing we have one life to live.

The bold and the beautiful are young and
    restless

so must take it easy or end up in general
    hospital or

another world with no

guiding light.

CHAPTER 12

THE START OF SOMETHING

By Cheryl "Shelley" Keeling

Running is the sweet spot where mind, body, and spirit convene to commune with God. It is an answer to grief, stress, obesity, bad health, and bad habits. It is a physical act that is a form of expression for something nonphysical such as pain, anger, or happiness. Running is an opportunity to connect with fresh air, the ocean, the trees, sunlight, and people—and disconnect from the shackles that bond us to an overregulated existence or less than exciting life. When running, one is free. It is a survival tool.

This attitude about running was the primary factor in a decision to enter my mother, then sixty-seven years old, in a 5K race after the brutal murders of both her sons within two years and eight months of each other. The loss of a child was not an uncommon occurrence in the St. Nicholas projects where we were raised or other low-income areas driven by a drug trade that was accompanied by crime and violence, death, destruction, and despair.

What was uncommon and very noticeable was the shell of the woman remaining after the deaths. Generally playful and full of life, Mom was in a downward spiral. Desperate to help Mom get her mind off the tragedies, I asked her if she wanted to run in a 5K race. She did not know that 5K means 3.1 miles. I felt certain she would finish without incident, and she did. This began a three-decade running career which would include five age-group world records in both indoor and outdoor track.

A track athlete moves to a new age group every five years. Mom began in age group 65–69 and has competed in eight different age groups with her most impressive accomplishments after 90 years old. Mother is a most remarkable human being. Now at 101 she still sets goals for herself and tests her strengths and abilities. She is a role model and inspiration for people of all ages.

"Miss Ida" as she is known in the world of track and field was always easy to coach. She did not mind that our roles had been reversed, and since she had always been very active, the tasks were welcomed and came easily to her. People sometimes find it hard to believe that my mother just took off running and won that very first time. They want to know if she underwent weeks of some kind of professional training. The truth is that it never occurred to me that she wouldn't be able to finish. Mommy was always athletic in some way. She taught us how to ride our bikes by pushing it and running behind us, and she was already in her forties at that time. She has told me that when she was a kid, she was the handball queen of her block and that no one (boy or girl) could beat her at the game. When my sister and I were children, Mommy walked us everywhere. It wasn't unusual for the three of us to walk forty or fifty blocks in one day.

None of this stopped her from pushing herself when it came to racing. She is her own toughest critic and had been bitten by the running bug. She has experienced the serenity and feeling of well-being that accompanies running. She commented that she had slept the best since the passing of my brothers the night of that first 5K race.

After a series of four and five-mile races over many years, I explained to Mother that we lose muscle mass as we get older. To stay strong for the outdoor season of road racing, we began competing on the track; to stay strong for the track, we began lifting weights. Mother always loved to go to the gym. She had many friends there and the new venue added a social aspect to the training which she loved. I could see she was now ready for an international meet. Mom was eighty years old. I entered her in the 800 meters—the half mile—in the age group 80–84. She finished third and brought the bronze medal home for the US. She was happy. I was beaming. The transformation seemed complete. Although nothing could bring my brothers back, I felt that Mom had climbed her way out of that dark hole. Now I knew it was time to really get busy.

Regardless of the distance, one must always have a plan. Those who fail to plan, plan to fail. The race plan must be within the physical capabilities of the body. Mom was training, running, racing, and I was watching and calculating. I decided the 800 and the 400 would be too stressful for Mom's tiny body. By ninety years old she was running the 100 meters outdoors and the 60 meters indoors. She was fine as long as she continued to medal, which was almost a certainty as there were few people her age racing. This brought her a Lifetime Fitness Award at the Atlanta Senior Games and a gold medal in the 100 meters.

As her coach, I looked at the race as ten 10-meter races, calculating each step, her arm movement, her breathing, the expression on her face. She too was calculating, but differently: Am I too tired, will I stumble, will I disappoint my family and friends? Even when the race is short, it is long!

In 2008, when Mom was ninety-two years and ten months, I asked her if she would like to go with me to France where I would be competing. She was excited about the opportunity, and off to the World Veteran Athletic Games we went. Clermont-Ferrand was where Mom set her first world record. We were now paying more attention to diet, making sure Mom had enough protein and calories. She always had healthy eating habits but now she was aware of how to tweak her eating for maximum benefit.

Mom caught the attention of the media after her indoor race at the armory in New York City. She had set a second world record at ninety-five years old. She has set a record every year except one since that time and has been featured on evening and morning television shows, on Lisa Ling, and in *Vogue*, *O* magazine, *Time* magazine, and many more. Her latest and most watched story and race was Penn Relays in April 2016, just a few weeks short of her 101st birthday. According to Noah Remnick (author of the feature) of the *New York Times*, mama's story received twenty million views in five days. He said, "It was the second most viewed article in the history of the *Times*."

She is not finished with us yet!

SOAPS

As the world turns with one life to live, we
must continue to make use of

the days of our lives.

General hospital is overcrowded with the young
and the restless.

Ryan's Hope left TV for another world in search
of tomorrow.

Meanwhile, all my children is looking for the
guiding light

before the edge of night.

[CHAPTER 13]

A LANE OF MY OWN

Do not cast me away when I am old.

—PSALM 71:9

At one hundred and two, I have more than earned the right to walk wherever I want, but I choose to run. For me, life's still a sprint. At the start of a February 2011 race, I stood sixty meters from my destination, clasped my hands over my head when I was introduced on the PA, then leaned forward with my right hand on my knee when the runners were told to get set.

The gun sounded, and I was off, putting to shame younger couch potatoes, excuse givers, or plain old slackers who might've been well accustomed to convincing themselves that they were too over the hill to compete. That's the thing about feeding yourself negative information. It always slows you down. I surged forward in my yellow shoes, salmon-colored shirt, and matching earrings.

Masters' Spring Night at the armory in Washington Heights was the place I most wanted to be as I ran again, proving that no amount of horrific loss in life was going to keep me isolated and in despair.

Loss in life is certainly not new. Loss as human beings age goes with the territory of traveling life's journey. Still, there are some losses that can break the spirit. There are losses that rob one of the will to live, scramble the mind and emotions, or produce a depressed stupor that becomes a safe haven for enduring grief.

For me, my tremendous faith in God and running, running, and more running keeps me connected, active, and, I hope, serves as a foundation to inspire others. I find running a very enjoyable thing.

Life can force you to become tough, durable, and determined. My memories of growing up in Harlem are fresh and clear and still shape my view of the world. I know that the world has kind, mean, nice, selfish, black, white, Asian, young, old, and every other kind of person you can think of. The key to happiness is to forget what folks look like. Just find the nice, kind, supportive people and bring them into your circle. Let the others find God in their own way and in their own time.

Back when I was young, many decades ago, life was generally hard for everyone who wasn't of means. For black people who were trying to survive the Great Depression, life was especially hard. However, I didn't let hardship change the way that I treated people, and I hope that you, the reader, will never disrespect your fellow men and women either. There is never an excuse for meanness.

I am healthy and strong. I can't remember the last time I was sick. There is more to me than meets the eye when you look at my eighty-three pound, four foot, six inch frame. Yes, I am very small. My running shoe size is only five and a half.

Tragedy is a friend to no one, but it was through tragedy that I, urged on by my devoted daughter, changed my life and stunned the world by literally running through my pain. Running in the hallways of my Bronx apartment, running on treadmills, lifting weights, and riding exercise bikes all have become part of the regimen that I use to keep myself in shape and my mind sharp.

Cheryl is a law-school graduate, businesswoman, and track coach. She has told reporters that I don't let anything keep me down. "It's so uplifting," Cheryl has said.

Reporters want to know what someone over one hundred years old does and eats to stay so active.

For me, it's quite simple. I drink a lot of orange juice.

My day-to-day routine follows a pattern that could help young people get healthier too. I'm in bed at nine and get up promptly at six. Before getting out of bed, I exercise because it makes me happy to be moving flat on my back. I move my arms and pull my knees clear up to my chest. Then I get up lickety-split, put on my slippers, and go to the bathroom for my morning ablutions. From the bathroom, I start my next set of exercises which includes squats, twists, turns, and toe touching. Afterward I ride a bike.

A US Army recruiting commercial from the 1980s proudly boasted when it came to soldiers in the Army, "We do more before nine a.m. than most people do all day." Clearly, the brass of the US Army has never met anyone like me.

Staying in the right lane and staying healthy for me means not only exercising regularly and the right way, but eating the right foods. I like a heavy breakfast because I'm rested. My mind is at ease, I'm relaxed, and it makes me feel good. My preferred breakfast is not for wimps. It could be the leftovers from a previous day's dinner or chops, bacon, eggs, beans, and rice. I think my Caribbean heritage comes through in my choice of breakfast food.

Once breakfast is over, I might have tea, cocoa, or just one cup of coffee. Back in 1972, a doctor told me that a drop of Hennessy is good for poor circulation. He said that if Hennessey is not available, then port wine will do. Hooray for that doctor!

At dinnertime, I might have cereal, wheat products with hard-boiled eggs, and orange juice. I also like carrots, beets, celery, cucumber, and lots of other vegetables.

My health regimen is not unusual and it's not new. Personal trainers, fitness experts, and health coaches all say that good nutrition, exercise, and lots of sleep are necessary for good health. I also stamp my feet a lot to ensure good circulation. I used to drink milk because it's good for muscle and system recovery after a workout, but I'm allergic to milk now. I don't eat my food with any sauces or seasonings, but olive oil and lemons are most welcome.

But my most important health tip that I can give anyone is this: Do not let anyone aggravate you to the point where you cannot eat.

Like President Barack Obama, I absolutely refuse to tolerate drama. I'm that way because without good health and a clear mind, you don't have anything.

I just don't have time for people who live only to cause trouble. I don't like to ask anyone for anything either. I wash, cook, iron, scrub, clean, mop, and shop. I don't want nobody helping me do nothing if I can do it myself.

I've run in short races. I've run in distance races. I'm a sprinter and world record holder in the ninety-and-over age group. I set a record of 31.80 seconds in the 60-meter run, but it was later broken. No matter, I just keep running.

Back when I was ninety-two, Cheryl and I went to France. I was competing in the World Athletic Veteran Games. (It's now called the World Masters Games.) We got there two days before the race and the hotels in the city of Clermont-Ferrand were all booked up. No problem. We flew into Paris and went to Lyon by car. It cost a lot of money but I was determined to compete in the race.

The hotel where we stayed was breathtaking. It was truly beautiful but I had to concentrate on my running, which was business. On the morning of the race, I woke up early, ate a big champion's breakfast, then took the train to Clermont-Ferrand. It was a four-hour journey, and I spent the time getting myself psychologically and emotionally prepared to give my all.

Finally, I arrived. An escort took us to the pre-race tent, and I started getting my mind and spirit ready for a great race. Then I heard the voice of the announcer. It was time for me to race. I was escorted out onto the track and into my lane for the lineup. All the runners were out there, looking intense, ready and anxious to get started. I was scheduled to run in the group for women who were 90–94 years old.

Before the gun was fired to start the race, the voice over the loudspeaker was informing the crowd in the stands of who the runners were and giving their ages. When people learned my age, the applause was lengthy and robust. I could not help feeling a warm sense of pride. I felt focused and nervous but I was also determined. In other words, I was ready.

The gun sounded, and when it was over I had won another race. The French media folks were so nice and made me feel like I had really accomplished something special.

I think that people like reading about me because everyone knows that as the years add up, people slow down. It's called aging. By the time a runner is over forty, they slow down by nearly two seconds for every mile.

Older runners have more difficulty accomplishing something known as "vertical push" off the ground because of decreased muscular power as compared to younger runners. The limiting effects of diminished "vertical push" mean that senior runners have to employ a greater, or higher, frequency of stride to run faster. While younger runners appear to be loping along with ease, senior runners are covering distances in what appears to be a shuffle. I don't mind though. Whatever works.

I've been told that senior runners also have to contend with what happens as a result of their heightened stride frequency. They say that higher frequency of stride leaves less time for achieving efficiency of movement. One of the best ways to fight against the combined effects of higher stride frequency and the inefficiency that comes with it, especially when running at higher speeds, is weight training to maintain muscle mass. I had to learn that an easy way to address loss of muscle mass is to adopt an appropriate program of weight training.

So for senior runners like me, the addition of years under-standably causes some changes, but there's good news. It turns out that for older runners like me, the higher frequency of stride produces less stress coursing through the body with each step. As a result, older runners have a lower incidence of running related injuries that can take down younger folks.

One of my most satisfying achievements happened when I beat my own record at the New York Armory Track and Field Center. I was shocked when reporters from ESPN, ABC News, the *Huffington Post*, and other places picked up the story.

Since I never set out to become even a little bit of a celebrity, God must have put me in this spotlight for a reason.

Many choose to ignore God or have concluded that there is no God. For me, God has been my living beacon of hope. Without God to guide me during my darkest days, I don't know what would have become of me.

The God that I have relied upon all the days of my life was with me when I lay keening for my mother after she died. That same God made sure that Laura and Cheryl escaped from a burning building. That same God kept me strong enough and healthy enough and blessed enough to get up every morning as I struggled to raise four children on my own. There were certainly times of despair and wondering if God heard my prayers. No despair or moment of wondering could last or triumph over the words God spoke in Hebrews 13:5 when the Creator of the Universe promised, "I will never leave you or forsake you" (NRSV).

Finding the determination to make it through every day while sewing in a factory so I could house, clothe, and feed my four children was helped by remembering the long night Jesus, the Christ, spent. In those harsh, lonely hours when the Lord knew that he'd been betrayed and that his time of trial and death would soon be upon him, Christ fell face first to the ground and pleaded to God, saying, "Father, if it is possible, may this cup be taken from me. Yet not as I will, but as you will."

God let my girls leave me and learn to live on their own while completing their studies. They came home at times. Eventually Laura decided that she wanted to live in South Carolina and she stayed there for a long time. Now, she lives in North Carolina. Laura is retired and she does volunteer work writing for many papers online.

Cheryl liked my place to be her home base but she moved around a lot. When she was young and in college, I told her that she has called me from very strange places but she just laughs and says things like, "Belgium isn't strange, Mom." She lives in New York City now where she has many jobs including one as head coach up at prestigious Fieldston School. Those kids are very happy and the parents love her very much. Also up at the armory, Cheryl trains folks in tennis and even started a camp with the children. That is why I don't like to bother her too much. She has so much to do and she's always in training for races too.

Recently, someone asked me what was the best decision I ever made in my life. It was to marry Lawrence Keeling. When we got married, we got along pretty good, but men have this crap in their heads that they never get out. They think guys will be guys which comes from boys will be boys, and that old stupid mentality even though people don't say it anymore, is still there. They are brought up to believe that they should get a pass no matter what they do. But, when I think back now, he was a wonderful man. He loved me. The last years of his life were pretty hectic but he would have been gratified to know how our two children turned out.

They are nice, intelligent, educated, and compassionate women. They made the right choices in life.

God's loving arms were there to catch me in the aftermath of the brutal drug-related slayings of my sons. The devastation of the murders was made worse by both cases going unsolved, and with the persistent encouragement of Cheryl, I found my way back into the land of hope *by running.*

Some might wonder how I could have found freedom in running. How could my heart have been healed by taxing it to work harder by running on tracks and trails? Like other areas of my life, and like other times when life has tried to steal my joy, I have relied upon my faith. At times, it's been difficult because, even by his own words, God has declared that there will be times when mere mortals simply will not know why their lives go in certain directions. There will be times when those of faith will wonder where the Great Maker was when darkness was closing all around and even the good will of family and friends could not stem the pain.

Some lives have more than their share of tragedy. There have certainly been people who have suffered far more than I have. Some become bitter and angry with God. They wonder why God withheld his mighty hand of power during moments of crisis. They rage and shake their fists at the sky. I don't do that. I have clung to God's reassurances that my Creator ultimately knows what's going on, and that, if I trust him all will be well.

I'm really enjoying my athletic career, and so far, I have nothing but pleasant memories about it.

Over the last couple of years, I've been surprised by all the razzle dazzle. Imagine me in *Vogue* magazine? I wonder what

Mama and Daddy would have thought about that. Sometimes all the razzle dazzle makes me wonder if I'm dreaming.

In the last few years, the *New York Times* and ABC News came calling to talk to me about my life and my running. No matter how many times it happens, I still can't believe that these great institutions are interested in talking to little old me. It's like getting a big hug that says it is okay to invest in hope especially when all you are feeling is despair. I hope that my refusal to sur-render to devastation, heartbreak, and aging will move someone else to do the same thing: find a way to get up and create a new, full life. While people are understandably left speechless by my accomplishments at this age, Cheryl feels that the significance of what I'm doing is not in breaking records but in setting them.

So far, I've won a medal and lifetime award for my partic-ipation in a race in Atlanta in 2005. I was ninety at the time. I followed that achievement in 2008 by setting a world record for runners in my age group while competing in Clermont-Ferrand, France. At a forever-young ninety-five years old in 2011, I set the world record for my age group by running 60 meters in 29.86 seconds at a Manhattan track meet. In 2012 at the USA Track and Field (USATF) Eastern Regional Open, I leaned forward into a 2.3 meter per second headwind and completed a 100-meter dash in 51.85 seconds. I'm surprised that some of my competitors included runners young enough to be my great grandchildren.

2014 proved to be another good year for me. In August of that year, at the age of ninety-nine, I participated in the Gay Games in Akron, Ohio. Running in the 100-meter dash, I set the record for people in my age group by completing the event in 59.80 seconds. I topped 2014's performance in 2016 when, on April 30, 2016,

I became the first female centenarian in history to complete the 100-meter run. My time was 1:17:33, and it was the best time ever recorded for any female one hundred years or older for that event.

None of this is easy for me. I have chronic sinusitis plus arthritis in my knees and toes. I also have arthritis in my hands and sometimes it hurts real bad, but I can't let it keep me down. I also have to do a lot of sewing. When I buy something, I have to fix it because I am so small. I find a way to do whatever I need to do. I can't let myself down.

I've been asked if I'm afraid of anything. Well, I go out by myself a lot because I'm an outdoor person and I also like to have some independence. For some reason, I've started worrying about losing my memory while I'm walking the streets alone, not knowing my name and unable to tell anyone where I live. When I start worrying about that, I force myself to dismiss it. I just write my name, address, and phone number on a card, put it in my pocket, and walk out the door. God will lead me home.

As much as I like to be independent, I do use common sense. There truly is no substitute for common sense.

In 1993, I was seventy-eight years old. It had become really scary around the St. Nicholas Houses and many other housing projects. Well before his difficulties with Watergate, President Nixon had declared a war on drugs. For New York, the kingpin of drugs was heroin. Perceived as a swamp of violence, corruption, and urban decay, the drug plague that hit New York City in the 1970s brought with it an astonishing escalation in violence. Riding the subways became particularly hazardous due to the assaults that took place in tunnels and on trains. People were mugged outside their apartments. Junkies shambled through the streets, imposing their desperate needs and ways on everyday citizens who struggled to survive the day.

The drug problem was out of control and the young people were beating and robbing the old people. In fact, there were far too many robberies right in my building. Harlem back in the late 1990s was much worse than it is now and the police couldn't keep up with the number of crimes. So when a friend of mine told me about a really nice, empty apartment at the Dorie Miller Houses in Corona, Queens, I decided to take it. I stayed in the Dorie Miller Houses for eight years and I was eighty-six years old when I moved again. I didn't let my age stop me at this latest challenge. I just stepped out in faith and believed that our Lord and Father would guide my footsteps into the right direction, and that is exactly what He did. This time I took an apartment in the Bronx that was very close to Cheryl.

One of my favorite stories is about the time I raced in France. It was 2008 and I was ninety-two years old. Cheryl went with me. On the way to the race I made sure that I was quiet so that I could get in the right mental space for racing. I didn't talk so I ended up napping on the train. When I got there and my race was called, I went to a certain spot and an escort took us into a pre-race tent and then I sat there and got nervous. Then an escort took me out on the track to my lane. I lined up there. I had to stand in a certain spot and they called your name out in the stadium and said how old I was. "Ida Keeling, USA!" I got a lot of applause. Then I just waited for the gun. The prerace feeling is a combination of pride, nerves, and intense focus. All you want to see is that finish line. The French newspapers wrote a lot about the whole race because of my age.

People that I have known for years always want to know if I've met this or that celebrity. It is nice to see these folks, and I don't ask for autographs, but I do let them know that I recognize their accomplishments and respect the journey they have taken and the impact they have made on the lives of others. People ask most about Oprah Winfrey and President Obama. I did not meet Oprah, but I have met her great friend, Gail King. I've met Lisa Ling and a few other people who are famous in the world of running, but I tell my friends that none of that matters. I didn't start running to meet celebrities; I had to do it to clear my mind.

The last poem I ever wrote was on the day after Barack Obama won the election. Here it is:

The New President Barack Obama

It's President Obama's time
with his beautiful family
decorating the White House in style.
He is a man for all seasons. A man of the world.
A concerned person for people everywhere.
His honesty and sincerity distinguishes his
    character.
This character that he wears like a badge of
    honor.
It's President Obama's time.
A man with a plan in hand to rid the world of
    political games
and injustices.

A plan to lift the lid off the coverups and clean
   up the mess
at last
which he inherited from the past.
It's President Obama's time.
Time to bring about world peace.
Our President who said, "Yes We Can."
With trust, togetherness and understanding
we will bring about world peace.
And a better tomorrow.
All the blessings of the world to you, Michelle,
   Sasha and Malia.

I never thought that I'd live to see a black man in the White House. I wonder what Mama and Daddy would have thought about that.

If I had my pick of famous people to meet, I would love to meet Michelle Obama and Barack Obama. He was the best president we ever had and Michelle was a great first lady. They made a great team. They really made the White House shine.

Cheryl threw me a one hundredth birthday party in May 2015 at a swanky restaurant in downtown Manhattan. There were ninety-five guests and it was wonderful to see my nephews and nieces whom I hadn't seen in many years. They were all grown up. When I last saw them they looked like children; now all the girls looked like somebody's mama. I just went up to each one of them and said, "Hi, nice to meet you," because I couldn't remember their names or which one of my siblings each one belonged to. Once they opened their mouths and began talking, I was able to figure it out, but I couldn't do it based just on how they looked. For example, the last time I'd seen my nephew Michael, he and his mama were getting in a car to go somewhere and he was about twelve and his sister was about ten, and now he was a man with children of his own.

I almost lived to see another miracle. A few days before the latest election, I was contacted by ABC to join a few other women to say a few words on camera. It was to be shown after Hillary Clinton won and became the first female president of the United States. Since she didn't win, the speech wasn't aired.

I'll never stop going to the gym. My gym will always be involved in my life. I will always allow time to work out at least two or three days a week. So, between cleaning up my home and doing my gym exercises, I don't have a whole lot of stamina left over. My energy is simply not what it used to be.

When I go to the gym, I see young people in their twenties and thirties trying to do simple things like push-ups and sit-ups. They sometimes have a hard time completing these activities because their bodies are not used to moving around a lot. At least, I think that might be the reason that they have to strain so hard. I hear them groaning and grunting as they try to make it to one hundred push-ups. Then they look at me sailing through my regimen and they come over to find out how I'm doing it at my age. Most of the time, they think that I am in my seventies. When I say that I'm over a hundred years old, their mouths drop open and they say things like, "Gee, how do you manage to move like that?" It really cracks me up.

When I have a race coming up, I take it a lot easier. I get more rest and stay out of the gym for just a few days. I am very much aware that I am old and there is no point in being foolish by going to the gym and then directly to a race. That just don't make no sense.

I know that my running will not spare me from more heartache or physical pain. I'm not trying to run from trouble. But as I run, it is my hope that others are watching my strides and will be encouraged, inspired, or motivated to do their own type of running, to pursue their own goals and not look back. I'm running toward solutions, strength, and hope. Every step that I took from my first competition to the present has been my way of declaring that nothing will keep me down.

I hope that my sharing this story will help someone embark on their own journey with a light in their eyes, or survive their troubles knowing that anything is possible if you just believe and keep the faith. There can not only be light at the end of the tunnel, but solace in the arms of God.

God has my back. So I keep running.

ABOUT THE AUTHORS

One hundred and two-year-old **Ida Keeling** is a mother, activist, and runner. Miss Ida, as she is known in her Bronx community, grew up the child of immigrants during the Depression. She began working to help provide for her family at age twelve. After her husband passed, she raised her four children alone while serving as an active member in the civil rights movement. She started running at sixty-seven years old to overcome the grief of losing her two sons. Today, Ida is a world-record holder for the 60-meter dash in the 95–99 age group and continues to set new records with each race. She has been profiled in the *New York Times*, *Vogue*, *Essence*, and on ABC News.

    Anita Diggs is the author of *The Other Side of the Game*, *A Meeting in the Ladies Room*, *A Mighty Love*, and *Talking Drums: An African-American Quote Collection*. She holds an MFA in Creative Writing and teaches at Salem College in Winston-Salem, North Carolina.